The

Universal

Religion

The Universal Religion

Essentials for a Joyful Life

Christopher Lepine

Revelation Publishing

The Universal Religion:
Essentials for a Joyful Life

By Christopher Lepine

Published by:

 Revelation Publishing
P.O. Box 7136
Newark, DE 19714-7136

Publisher's Cataloging-in-Publication Data

Lepine, Christopher
    The universal religion: essentials for a joyful life /
    Christopher Lepine. — 1st ed.
       p. 256 ; cm. 1.59 — (The universal religion ; 1)
    Includes bibliographical references.
    LCCN: 99-90736
    ISBN 0-9634081-1-9 (pbk.: alk. paper).
    1. Religions (Proposed, universal, etc.) 2. Spiritual life 3. Urantia
    book I. Title.
BL390.L57 1999   299'.93
                                                   QBI99-959

To Ellen, my wife who supports me in great love
and wisdom, and continually walks with me
through the wonder of God's love.

Acknowledgements

O

Finally, a longstanding personal ambition has been realized—this book. It's been a work which has evolved over some years and is the product not only of my efforts, but those of the many family, friends, and associates who helped at each step of its evolution. Therefore, it's not only the creative work of my mind, but that of the many minds who cheerfully assisted.

Very Special thanks goes to my wife for her belief in this project and editorial advice, to Larry Mullins who offered continued style and formatting suggestions, to Jill Hull who heartily reviewed and read early versions for editorial correction and encouragement, and to the several pre-press reviewers who provided suggestions to further refine the book.

Also, I must thank the numerous individuals who kindly offered their valuable time to be interviewed, those who shared their thoughts, experiences, and deep feelings. These people invited me into their homes and businesses to ask difficult questions in the midst of a busy day or a stressful time of life. The material in this book could not have been illustrated as well without the help of the interviewees, for they provided the *real* examples of spirituality.

Next, of course, I owe a great deal to the authors, leaders, and livers of true religion and enlightened philosophy. These people from our history sing the same song of spiritual vision that leads us on to destiny and the fulfillment of our highest ideals. While it's easy to outline and emphasize the differences between religions, belief systems, and cultures, reading the sayings and thoughts of the great religious leaders helped me amplify my points of a universal religion.

And, I must not forget the tremendous debt I owe to the authors of *The Urantia Book*. This work provides the inspiration for a universal religion, and is thus, an invaluable beacon for my book as well as my spiritual thinking.

Finally, my most humble and gracious thanks goes to God, the real star of this book. From the beginning to the end, He provided all, even before I knew what I needed or where I was going. I suppose it's always like that.

Contents

O

Contents

Introduction

O

You're in the store or perhaps somewhere else, either looking for a friend or yourself, and have unknowingly selected a book of great import. Whether you grabbed it from among the multitude for its cover or title, I'm pleased and thrilled to have the opportunity to share an *amazing* discovery and set of principles to help you achieve continual transformation.

This experience can occur daily and has the potential of invigorating your soul and bringing you to the beginning of your *true destiny* as well as inspiring your family, friends, and acquaintances to acts of greatness and nobility. This most valuable of truths will fully satiate every good desire of your soul and bring you unimagined heights of new opportunity and enduring joy. And just as you are destined to realize these truths (through this book or another source), humankind is also poised for a universe destiny in philosophy, science, and religion. Indeed, all of us are touching the shores of an undreamed-of land and a full understanding of The Universal Religion.

Like most seekers, I too have plumbed the resources of the written word and have been frustrated by the forest of information that can brutally oppress and overwhelm the search for truth and the realization of spiritual longing. We don't go out and invest significant quantities of time and resources just for the immediate value of experiencing a book, group, speaker, talk show, or therapist. No, each of us *craves* the completion of self, the experience of God, the association of our fellows, and the joy of service. These threads unify the spiritual and religious expressions of humankind and remain the acid test for any experience or approach to personal spiritual experience. We are inexorably stretched to find completion by satisfying our constant yearnings for growth and God and *will not* experience real peace or progress until we understand the basic truths of God, the universe, ourselves, and our friends; until we accept reality, we cannot live.

This has always been the story of humanity, but now, in these first moments of the millennium, we demand help! We cry and agonize for our unmet longing and shove the meaningless explanations and priorities of our confused era over the precipice to avoid going into that same dead pit. Our hearts are *open* for the real thing. And because we've finally opened our hearts, they can be touched, caressed, and soothed by a gentle hand beckoning to the world of light and life: the Creator.

This book is a culmination and encapsulation of my understanding of the most profound and valuable spiritual resource I've found among the monolith of books, tapes, etc. *The Universal Religion: Essentials for a Joyful Life* is inspired by *The Urantia Book* and amply supported by quotations from our great religious traditions as well as contemporary expressions. This is truly a book which you can integrate with your present valued truths (in a religious tradition or otherwise) because it places ageless truths in a new context and unifies them around the basic overarching truths of The Universal Religion. It is these universal truths which will unify humankind and get you charged up and excited about life.

The text is open, plain, and meaningful, brimming with powerful insights and useful techniques for furthering the spiritual life. The chapters are arranged in a logical sequence where the basic foundation truths lead easily one to the next, until the whole of the spiritual life is illuminated, combining the best of the Eastern and Western approaches. You can know God as a person and friend while enjoying the experience of contacting His Spirit and seeking guidance.

In addition, every chapter teems with examples and anecdotes of first-hand spirituality from ordinary people, not noted authorities or public figures. You'll be able to think about a concept and then see how others articulate and live it in the "real world." After I completed the first draft of the manuscript for this book, a friend suggested I integrate interview material from all kinds of people in various stages in life. As I went to my friends and acquaintances asking questions, I discovered their remarkable and original insights, all reflective of The Universal Religion. Each has poured his or her heart out for our benefit. I owe them a great deal.

I believe wholeheartedly that the statements in this book are true and the best synthesis of Eastern and Western approaches and will lead you to unknown avenues of spiritual satisfaction. My life has known the depths of total black despair and the heights of luminescent joy. Twenty years ago I decided to test the truths in this book with life's demands. My daily experience, as well as much that I've read, has only confirmed and strengthened my core beliefs. My purpose is to share them and encourage you to accept the experiences that will develop as you read the book. **Your wholehearted open-minded reading of this book and use of its principles and techniques will bring you solid spiritual sustenance and ever-increasing joy.**

This book is designed to take your heart and mind on a journey of spiritual progress which will never end. I promise you that your total dedication to truth and openness of heart will be rewarded by these pages. Much of what you will read you may have heard before. However, the total focus of your will on the core teachings will confirm that this book has a profound recipe for God-consciousness and that it has a new view of spirituality.

So, allow yourself to go through this step-by-step journey to unseen wonders. Give me the pleasure of transporting you to a place you may never have seen or helping you to explore it more if you've been before. You may be tempted to rush over sections you feel are old hat, but *the presentation of the material is almost as important as its content.* Be patient and enjoy, even if you feel you are a pro.

I ask, friends, that you join me with an open heart, "Come as a little child," and experience the fresh, pure, invigorating wind, the breath of the Creator, and live as a progressive adult to triumph and thrive on all life's experiences. Let's go together and examine these truths. With pure wholeheartedness and sincerity, a hunger for the truth, and the faith to accept what comes to light, please allow me to share that which meets the desire in my heart and the yearnings of my soul.

May you find this within these pages . . . The Universal Religion.

That which the world needs most to know is: Men are the sons of God, and through faith they can actually realize, and daily experience, this ennobling truth.

Jesus, from *The Urantia Book*

It's Not Too Good
To Be True

The Real Adventure
Chapter 1

O

My friend, I have the pleasure of humbly sharing with you the *greatest* piece of knowledge in the universe. It can transform and electrify your life with the thrill of growth and the hope for improvement in *any* situation. This is the Universal Religion, not merely an endless existence of dull ease, but one beyond our greatest hopes and conceptions of happiness, opportunity, satisfaction, and adventure.

The words spiritual, God, faith, and service make many people recoil and still more avoid an examination of life's meaning and their destiny. We avoid these words because we cringe at the self-righteous, the hypocritical, the self-satisfied, and the greedy who use them as props and façades. But, we also listen to those who say these experiences are an illusion, a pointless fantasy of the weak and self-indulgent.

Now it's time to claim what's ours, our birthright as women and men, children and adults! We want to know the truth. Sure, we've had bad experiences, but why should we close our minds? We won't be robbed again, but instead, we'll know the truth and take the steps to eternity.

This brightest truth dwarfs the discoveries of science, the creations of our imaginations, and the grandeur of true art. This fact is the center of all that's been, is, and ever will be —eternity. It is the supernal release of the true, beautiful, and good in the expression of a meaningful human life. Even the most fantastic, imaginative, or hopeful assertion cannot approach or begin to equal this fact, this living experience of the highest kind.

You are a child of a perfect Father-God!

We're the children of God who don't need middlemen or phonies. What we *do* need are all well-meaning seekers of truth whatever their religion or belief system. Let's honor and support each other's sincere quests since we're all sons of God on the mission of eternal existence.

"Sonship" and "sons of God" are broad phrases signifying the intimate origin we have in the Creator and the intimate relationship we have with Him. This term isn't meant to signify the gender of those who are called the "sons of God" but their *origin* in the Father. Whether a man or woman, girl or boy, we're all "sons of God."

To begin, we must remember that this sonship derives from several facts. Firstly, we are all sons of God because we are His offspring. Further, we're sons of God because we can use our *faith* to realize it. In addition, we're sons of God since a divine son of God became one of us and unifies us with his Spirit. Lastly, we're sons of God because the Father gives us our unique selfhood and freewill, plus His Spirit living within.

For all who are led by the Spirit of God are sons of God. For you did not receive the spirit of slavery to fall back into fear, but you have received the spirit of sonship.

When we cry, "Abba! Father!" it is the Spirit himself bearing witness with our spirit that we are children of God.

The Bible

In the end, we're simply the children of God, the family of God, the friends of God, His offspring, His beloved.

Visualize a comfortable and secure home with a man, a woman, and their baby sitting on a couch. The couple looks with satisfaction at their creation, their child, a spark of new life, a gentle voice. Completely dependent, this infant is taken care of and will continue to be; each parent makes it their joy, their privilege to raise this baby. There is no sacrifice too painful, nor effort too large these parents won't make. This is a family.

Imagine yourself as this child and God taking the role of the parents. Since the divine Father is your parent He provides for all your needs before you realize you have them —before you ask Him. Comprehend that it's this way now and for good, despite what happens or how much you change. This is the greatest spiritual treasure: It's yours for the asking.

"The kingdom of God is within you" was probably the greatest pronouncement Jesus ever made, next to the declaration that his Father is a living and loving spirit.

The Urantia Book

Our needs *are* the yearnings and desires for a better life, undeniable and ever-present. Added to these, we must simultaneously cope with inherent personal imperfections and outer problems. The only way to fulfill these needs and solve these problems is by seeking God and living with Him. Our loving Father saves us from our limitations to free us for unending spiritual achievement.

Everything you don't like about your behavior can be overcome through cooperation with God, using unpleasant experiences as *opportunities* for growth, the way they should be used. While God creates us as raw potential, He also gives us the thrill of endless growth, the greatest gift. This transcends all suffering and problems. Your divine Father will deliver you from your limitations if you use faith to solve problems and reach goals, even in the thick of personal agony or apparent hopelessness.

> *How grateful I am to Amida, who thought to provide for the salvation of one so helplessly lost . . .*
>
> Shinran

Experiencing Your Birthright

If you sincerely want to know the truth, listen with an open mind and believe what you're experiencing. You'll know you're a child of God by your faith. The process will begin because you've listened, acted with faith. The Spirit of God puts this experience of kinship with God in your mind already: It's pulsating continually, as real as any experience —indeed, the most intense experience of all! But, it's not obvious, not immediately experienceable.

Our minds block off this experience of God because we simply don't believe what we're experiencing, burying and explaining it away, saying it's not possible or real. We ignore and deny the experience of God because we've been told it's not real or attainable.

Consider this person's revelation:

> I was probably ten or eleven, and it was a nice day. I was what was called a milk boy in Catholic grade school, and I was wheeling a huge carton of empty milk

bottles around the building. I was just sort of exhilarated by the day plus the fact that I got out of class to do this. But suddenly it dawned on me that I was one of the luckiest kids on the planet because God loved me and I was one of His children. I can even remember laughing out loud just before the amazing tinkle of broken glass shattered my ecstasy. I had forgotten about the cart completely and there were broken milk bottles everywhere and I was immediately brought back to earth.

That was really my first awareness that I had this special place in God's heart . . . In college after Viet Nam, it was like you picked up from the day you left off; there was no gap at all; all of a sudden you realize this same sense of joy but in a broader more expanded way, that you're this same child of God, not only that, but so is everyone else. And the real spiritual astonishment from validating that in your soul and in your heart is the experience that you live on this planet for.

Imagine you'd like to get to Seattle, Washington and ask me what I know about it. After I've praised the attractions, emphasized the prominent features, and recommended going there, you'd probably want to know how to get there, even though you can't prove I'm telling the truth. Of course you've seen pictures and heard all about it, *but* you have not experienced it first hand.

After a while, after thinking about it and seeing it in your mind, you decide to believe what I say, although you still don't know if it's true. You make arrangements to go to Seattle . . . Upon returning from your trip, you've experienced the pleasures of Seattle and know them to be fact, the truth. You are now in the position I was.

You had a *sincere desire* to know the truth about Seattle, experience it first hand, and believed what I told you to be a possibility. To experience this truth, you had to act, had to do something and use your *faith* to get to Seattle. Finally arriving in Seattle, your belief became a *fact*, a direct experience, a personal truth because you accepted your experience.

To find and experience God, you must go through the same process. If you sincerely want to know the truth, use your faith—your persistent effort—and find God first-hand.

Take time each day to be alone, listening for the truth. Close your eyes and say everything that's on your mind; express your desire to know the truth. Pour your heart out! Do this with absolute intensity and listen. Eventually, you'll know you're a child of God because you've allowed God to get through.

When you recognize this experience, say that you believe it. Dedicate some time each day to practicing this spiritual exercise to draw strength and get guidance. This will direct and nourish your cycle of spiritual growth for as long as you desire.

> *When men and women ask what shall we do to be saved, you shall answer, Believe this gospel of the kingdom; accept divine forgiveness. By faith recognize the indwelling spirit of God, whose acceptance makes you a son of God.*
>
> Jesus, from *The Urantia Book*

The Outgrowths of Your Birthright

Think of it! For the entire history of humanity the immense majority of people haven't believed they could know God first-hand. Few ever thought this could happen daily just by releasing sincerity and faith. They either believed it wasn't possible or that an intermediary was needed between themselves and God.

It's time we realize our Father wants us to know Him one-to-one, not only through churches, nations, or organizations. If you act with vigorous faith you'll have what few have known, a personal spiritual experience based on and guided by your Universal Father.

Why not extend yourself to begin an upbeat life of unlimited progress? Find dynamic courageous living to the fullest. You don't need to go to a seminar, follow a leader, rely on others for truth, or search anywhere but the marrow of your being for **the source**. You don't need to exercise, restrict your thinking, study long hours, or seek outside authority figures. Your hand is already on the handle of the vault of panoramic brilliance. Dare to trust yourself and try, to risk what you believe and how you live, to open up to the life of your dreams.

> *Did you ever hear of a man who had striven all his life faithfully and singly toward an object and in no measure obtained it? If a man constantly aspires, is he not elevated?*

> Henry David Thoreau

Who can deny you this birthright? What can alter this divine fact? You who experience anger and fear, frustration and failure, confusion and doubt, longing and searching, who are abused, who hate yourself or feel guilty, who are depressed and lack self-esteem, who are proud and resist change, who are young, vibrant, and glowing, who are old and have plumbed the depths of a life experience, you who are despised, if you seek you will find.

Everyone comes from different ways of life, yet we're the children of God, a family. The findings of science, the intellectual gymnastics of philosophy, the confusion of cults, institutions, organizations and governments *will not* rob you of your birthright. You are a child of God. Absolutely nothing that's happened can change this fact. There is no way to erase this divine gift of life!

But again, we have to make the key decision, here or hereafter. **Without believing you're a child of God, there can be no spiritual progress, a relationship with God. Therefore, God will resurrect you after death to give you**

full opportunity to recognize this fact if you don't do this on earth and still crave truth and progress. Our loving Father looks at our hearts first and resurrects everyone who's sincere and has any amount of faith. There's no place called Hell or place of punishment, only a place to grow.

However, if we have erased our souls through neglect and apathy, selfishness and destructiveness, and/or intentional evil, God will be unable to resurrect us since we will have already destroyed the very vehicle of such a resurrection. Truly, "if you don't use it, you will lose it."

> *And it is not so much what mind comprehends as what mind desires to comprehend that insures survival; it is not so much what mind is like as what mind is striving to be like that constitutes spirit identification. It is not so much that man is conscious of God as that man yearns for God that results in universe ascension. What you are today is not so important as what you are becoming day by day and in eternity.*
>
> *The Urantia Book*

To say we're the children of God means we're the direct result of God's intention for us to live: We have a purpose in living and a value in advancing and may strive to imitate our Creator. Obviously we'll never become gods, but surely we can become more like God in the way we live.

We are sons and daughters of God! We have no limit to our destiny in relation to adventure, greatness, triumph, glory, satisfaction, nobility, courage, and achievement. We will perfect our individual purposes for living. You can do it. We can do it.

And please don't forget that God lives within you and is immediately available. Just make a sincere effort to talk to him, to know him. Doesn't a true parent wish to speak with his or her children? doesn't a true parent want the best for them and go to any length for their benefit and real welfare?

This is a fact for you, since you're a child of a loving and divine parent.

This person put it this way:

> God never makes you dangle on anything, but it seems like a spiritual guiding force . . . a fragment of God . . . and because I am who I am and what I am, resistant and stubborn and stupid as I am, sometimes I am guided, I am allowed to just run my course until I finally hit a wall. But when I come out of it I have grown a great deal because I have really gone to the depths. Spirituality is very, very real for me, very, very real. And it's unfortunate I think, that I have to have these two poles that I'm continuously bouncing back and forth . . . There has to be a middle ground there. Maybe I'll reach it one day. But when I am in tune, my spiritual reality is very, very real, and very tangible.

God's Desire for You

You see, *no matter what*, God wants you to begin this exultant adventure with Him. He asks only for your sincerity in wanting this relationship. Everything that's happened before doesn't affect your right to accept the eternal invitation to an eternal life of joyous achievement and stupendous intrigue.

The minute you decide (regarding admission into this process) the slate is clean; nothing can halt you except insincerity; the past has no bearing on God accepting you, the level of your present sincerity does. If you accept the truth of your origin in God, the evolution begins. God welcomes and forgives you.

Imagine you're walking down a long gray empty road, holding sacks of possessions in each hand, fighting against a stiff, bitter cold wind. You sit down for a rest and try to remember how you got here and what you're looking for. Despite your efforts, you have no answers. Your attention shifts to a house a close by. You hear laughter and see bright, colorful light coming through its windows.

Gradually you want to knock at the door to get inside, but fear rejection. You first approach it and rap quietly, timidly, then loudly. As it opens you see a room filled with people having a good time. An older couple stands at the door and says "Hello! Please come in; join us; the more the merrier." You've at last found what you desired. Surely these people can help. You know it's going to be alright.

And so it is; believing you're a child of God is simple and attainable, but requires old conceptions about yourself in the world to be abandoned. God waits by the side for us to stop our frenetic lives and join Him in genuine living. He signals us to believe with faith and experience the joy and certitude of being a child of God. Nothing is more comforting, more assuring, than to know what's always been true. No amount of optimism or logical deduction can replace the invigoration of your gift of kinship with God.

Only sincerity, a hunger for truth, and faith in the truth is necessary. **Nothing else is required to experience your birthright.** If you turn these keys in your mind now, you'll experience God and your kinship with Him and humanity. Our profound Father will go to all lengths to find and fellowship you, touch and illuminate you, comfort and heal you, talk with you, and know you—love you. God has forgiven you.

The Significance of Your Birthright

I believe many times we don't see the significance and uplifting meaning of our sonship with the Father, as though it's out of our range of vision, or beyond our reach. How untrue! The impact of this kinship with God is the greatest and truest of all experiences. It's the foundation of our personal and collective living habits and final destiny.

The birth of galaxies, the evolution of the myriad forms of life, the falling leaf, the cresting wave, the emergence of humankind, the development of civilization, the beauty we create, our achievements, are insignificant compared to a relationship with our Father. Your birth, first accomplishments, first love, later career success, recognition of your skill, popularity with friends, how could these take precedence over your potential experience of God? Our most valued human achievements and the wonders of nature are only glimpses of glory.

This doesn't discount the triumphs of humanity, nor lessen the magnificence of nature, nor extinguish individual achievement, but shows that the source of what we value and hold meaningful is our sonship with the source of the universe. All happiness, comfort, and great things radiate from the central truth of having a divine parent. While most of the world's pain and trouble are the product of humankind's mistakes or malevolence, the genuine splendors are only possible because you're a child of God.

Therefore, all fruitful things are possible from our birth in the Father. Without this knowledge we begin to resemble so many dying leaves. Life doesn't matter; people don't matter; only material things have importance. Soon, forgetting the gift of sonship, we become lost in a marsh, a wilderness of pleasure-seeking and ego-gratification. Exhaustion sets in and a realignment must be made. *We must accept God as Father for any kind of a bright and rewarding future.*

You were always a child of God, but acceptance of this fact makes the experience of kinship with God *experienceable*, a spiritual fact you'll notice to the depths of your mind. You are a child of God without experiencing it, but feel like an orphan without believing it. Dare to contact the truth. Nothing is more important than this first step of faith to spiritual liberty.

Serving Each Other to Grow

Anything is within our grasp, that is, anything that's true, beautiful, and good for us. If your goals and ideals are in accord with the divine Father's will, be assured that one day they'll be real. However, you must *participate fully* to accomplish them. This is spirituality.

Let's not forget friends, family, and the rest of humanity. Not only are there limitless possibilities for fulfilling your dreams and ideals, but intertwined is the constant need to better serve others, to do something for them to improve their lives and lighten their load—something they want done. This is also spirituality.

Realizing this, we accept life as a dance of interdependence where we grow by effectively doing the Father's will. We make use of our gifts in relationships that are ends in themselves, expanding with infinite possibilities. Although greatness awaits you, you must grow by using your courage and industry in honestly trying to live a good, enduring life. You must sweat and stretch to find happiness, notwithstanding that so many people are searching for a life of total comfort and ease. How could any of us expect God to dish up satisfaction without effort and progress, without faith? God is not a spiritual pizza driver!

Here's another lesson learned:

> Getting over this huge emptiness that I've had inside since my husband's death, that emptiness, that void . . . I thought it needed to be filled with another significant other relationship. That was something I think I was reaching out and searching for, a whole lot. After my experience with going for a relationship that seemed like it might work and be right, and it not being right, coming to the conclusion that that isn't life; that isn't everything; that that isn't going to be fulfilling. The fulfillment comes from day to day communication with, first of all, the Father: If you just dedicate every day as you wake up to

doing God's will and finding God's will. That's the most ultimately joyful thing in my life right now.

I feel like it's helped eliminate that void that I felt before. Realizing that I can be more loving and giving to friends and family and not need one significant person to give all my love to. In fact, that's something that my husband's death even taught me: You can't give all your love to just one person. You have to give it, feel it, like Jesus would have felt it more, for the whole human race.

I feel like I have a better life now than before.

We are interlaced with our companions, daily contacts, and family members, who guide and share our lives, all bringing avenues for friendship and association in the grand purpose of knowing God by serving others. Irritations and frustrations caused by individual differences are doors to growth and love as we push our limits. The journey wouldn't be possible if we didn't help each other move forward. This quest is based on the fact of a universal family.

A Creed

There is a destiny that makes us brothers;
None goes his way alone:
All that we send into the lives of others
Comes back into our own.

I care not what his temples or his creeds,
One thing holds firm and fast —
That into his fateful heap of days and deeds
The soul of man is cast.

Edwin Markham

The journey of spiritual growth immediately brings benefits in this life! In fact, eternal life is an extension and progression of the spiritual experiences we have here. We don't believe in God just to get to heaven, but to be empowered to start this moment to act lovingly and

dauntlessly. This pilgrimage is an adventure of progress, a tour of eternal life.

Finding Eternal Life

You are a child of God and ensure eternal life by making progress. If you genuinely desire a career of growth and helping others, you'll be awakened on the next world to pick up where you left off at death. Our loving divine parent provides a place to continue our steps toward Him through perfecting our ways of living.

Superior to your experiences, endowments, or beliefs, *your heart is the ticket to forever.* If you want to grow and help others, even if it's a fledgling faith, be assured you'll arise again and have eternal life. You will know yourself, meet old friends, and begin the fascinating exploration. Nothing in the universe can change this fact.

Frequently, understanding life after death is complicated by rules, creeds, belief systems, and doubts. But it doesn't matter what you believe to be received on the next shore, only the presence of faith and sincerity is necessary. Your religion, lack of religious membership, political party, race, status in life, or deeds, won't bar you if in your heart you're striving to become more by assisting others and growing.

> *To see a man fearless in danger,*
> *Untainted by lust,*
> *Happy in adversity,*
> *Composed in turmoil,*
> *And laughing at all those things*
> *   which are either coveted or feared by others —*
> *All men must acknowledge,*
> *   that this can be nothing else but a beam of divinity*
> *   animating a human body.*
>
>   Seneca

While your deeds, thoughts, and belief systems determine your spiritual progress and happiness here on earth, even if you didn't do much spiritual living, God is continually poised to give you a chance for a life of eternal adventure and delectable discovery after death. Despite mistakes you've made, however you see yourself, even if others despise you, the Father will take you in if you are sincere.

People say many things. They may insist there's one religion to join—theirs, or that you must subscribe to human authority to make yourself worthy for God. The very way you live may be molded and forced a certain way, along distinct lines by an organization or group that says this is the price for God and eternal life. Certain foods and exercise habits may be said to enhance your soul's chance of moving on to the joys of an afterlife. Workshops and seminars of all kinds are touted as improving your spiritual chances. And guess what? All of us have succumbed at times to these admission prices formulated by man to control man. You're not alone if you were told a certain fee was collected at the portals of heaven.

Just listen to this message found in a magazine: "There are many teachers of meditation. Only the enlightened offer the direct experience through their elevated presence. This is the mark of the masters."

Forget it all!!! —the unneeded and unnecessary requirements and guidelines for eternal life. Many of these activities improve your level of happiness, and even knowledge of God, but **no one can take away or replace the love of the Universal Father for His children!!!** If you honestly want to join the family of our Father, consider it done. God will carry you to the next world if you say "yes."

I think you'd agree that silly and over-complicated rules for eternal life and spirituality are those of humans in their efforts in the sincere search for God. A loving Father wouldn't make the path to eternal life so complicated and hard to find, so absurd. God's way is refreshingly fair and attainable by everyone in his or her own style. The Father that IS embraces people coming in the sincerity of service to others and eternal growth in knowing Him. This makes sense.

Your Progress and Destiny

This means that as a child of God you're striving and destined to become more like God in the ways you live. It's of a certainty we won't be equal to God, but our decisions and thoughts will endlessly improve. In trying to mirror God, it's obvious we've quite a long way to go, a process of growth that's endless. We'll always have infinite possibilities for striving, attaining, learning, loving, and enjoying the benefits of work.

Any destiny we pictured as ideal pales in the face of the wondrous universe that welcomes us. The longings and desires for good things, achievement, improving the world, helping others, getting to know God, and exploring the cosmos, were put there by the all-knowing One. Surely He'll provide us unlimited opportunities for satisfying them *all*. Remember, this is a fair universe.

Undoubtedly, certain ways of living and believing are better regarding spiritual progression and happiness; **there is a better and good way to live:** Everything is not relative; there are absolutes for truth, beauty, and goodness. These habits of living (of the spiritual life) must be addressed and honed, cherished and admired, and most of all valued, since without them, life becomes confused and complicated with problems unsolved, love unrealized—happiness lost. The key to cultivating these habits will be your sincerity, hunger for truth, and the faith to act in the process of serving others.

We progress through hard work, courage, discipline, and dedication, not through seeking a blissful, nonstop free ride to Paradise in the clouds. Eternal life is filled with pleasant friendships, good times, adventures, delightful pleasures, sublime ecstasy, great satisfaction, and tremendous happiness, a rhythm of work and play, change and stability.

The spiritual life is challenging and will require all you can muster for the journey, but never more than you can handle. Everything you need is there when you need it, in the way you need it.

Doubts, Fears, and Hesitation

It seems as though this is too good to be true; we don't think being a member of God's family is so simple. Receiving the greatest spiritual treasure just by sincerity in serving others seems ridiculous; it sounds a little too simplistic.

People may say this life with God is desirable but unattainable (Who would pass up the rewards if they were attainable and accessible?). They insist the world is a cold harsh reality of pain, suffering, evil, and confusion. And certainly, someone would declare that if you don't acknowledge these realities, you're setting yourself up for a big disappointment to your fantasies of God's land. Some people see religion as inconsequential, needing to be left behind in the progress of science and psychology.

In addition, our past experience shouts that nothing is easy—how could it be so simple to get into this spiritual family? When we look at some demanding human institutions and their admissions standards it's apparent only the cream of the crop is accepted. The professions and trades that serve us so well are built on excellence and don't have the lax admissions standards our Father has.

Isn't the spiritual supposed to be extremely special? It seems that something as important as eternal life and being a child of God should have walls just as high, important, discerning, and demanding.

Being Ashamed of Yourself

For most of us, it just seems we don't deserve it, not having lived lives that even come close to a spiritual ideal. It's easy to see how great leaders helping people, Gurus or Monks, or other spiritual specialists, could get these stunning treasures. It's very difficult to feel that simple people like ourselves are destined for such greatness and welcomed with open arms automatically.

If that's not enough, surely our many mistakes and insincere decisions should bar us, stain our admission card for kinship with God. We stop and think of things we've done to ourselves or others that we consider mean, evil, or immoral. Everyone can find many examples bearing this out.

Does this sound familiar?:

> I'd love to say . . . after I've recognized the realities of spirituality, that every day is bliss. Not so. My spiritual life is purely a roller coaster. And I'll go through long periods of time where God is *not even in my mind*, **at all**, I mean long periods of time. Maybe it's my character, maybe it's my nature, I have to go through these things in order to arrive at a real stability, spiritual stability.
>
> But for me, when I am on a downswing, when I'm not experiencing, when I'm not recognizing, when I'm not disciplining . . . (And to me, my religious life, discipline is part of it, I must sit down.) If I don't sit down with God every day, or very, very frequently, I'm on that downswing.
>
> The thing that brings spirituality to a climax for me is when I finally one day, for the forty-fourth time (My God, how many times do you have to go through it before you get it?!) . . . all of a sudden you decide to get back into it and everything lifts, your whole life, your whole . . . your psyche, is just elevated. And I just wonder . . . *what is wrong with me?* I know what I know; I experience what I experience spiritually, yet I can go through these downswings.
>
> I don't think that I'm unique there. I don't think that most people are content. Maybe they are. Maybe my life

is too chaotic; maybe I'm too resistant; maybe it's a lot of things. But when I'm in a spiritual mode, when I discipline, when I spend time with God, my God, my Father, daily, my life reflects it. My psyche reflects it . . . *I reflect it*. It's as simple as that. But boy when I'm not, when I'm on a down, I am the pagan of pagans. And it's incredible what you can justify . . . like I never heard of God.

How can we forget the numerous times of indecision and inaction, lives filled with failures to do what's right to help a friend or improve our world, not to mention ourselves? We appear to be manufacturers of missed opportunities, mistakes, cruelty, and confusion. How could God take us in with such a marred record? It seems we don't deserve what God has to offer us.

And most of all, we grasp for settled and predictable lives. We want relief. It's a struggle to keep on track and get by: This is a tough place. *Why should we take the risk of spirituality* when we can't rely on other people or events to turn out the way we thought they would, the way we thought they should? Why invite more stress?

The faith-risk of spiritual life, this sudden trust in the unseen God, means entering a different life of uncertainty and more challenges. How can we be sure everything will be alright? We crave concrete examples and guarantees to show us something may be gained.

These concerns and fears are real and make absolute sense to our minds, minds born of an evolutionary struggle that took billions of years. Ancient instincts grumble deep inside us, protecting against all change and seeking preservation at *any* cost. But, there's also singing in us a part of God showing glimpses of the celestial life, a life transcending the animal mind by helping here in this world.

This is the point of doubt that comes before experiencing a spiritual life of fullness. That is, it's time to act on spiritual leadings and do what your heart is telling you to do. This will mean a completely new life in the old world—you'll be changed, be required to do more, and led into trouble. You'll have to risk and sacrifice your certainty for the journey. This is a life of faith and cannot be had without the willingness to act on spiritual leadings.

Ultimately faith is the only key to the universe. The final meaning of human existence, and the answers to questions on which all our happiness depends cannot be reached any other way.

Thomas Merton

Your Value to God

It may be hard to acknowledge, but God needs *you*. He needs you to help Him touch the lives of His children: your family, friends, and fellow human beings. Moreover, your life has a value and greatness because of your origin in Him.

You may think you aren't worth much or don't have the ability to succeed or look back and see nothing but depressing failures. However, your life is a gift meant for happiness, the gift of sonship. **God wants you to be happy through helping Him with your will:** You were designed for it!

In the creation of your unique person, God provides abilities that no one has in the way you have them. But most of all, in the vast universe of creation, in all the countries of the world, looking at your city, there's only one you. Your unique personality has a purpose and place that's *needed*: That's why you're here. You too are as valuable as anyone whom you admire. We are original expressions of the Father as His children, and have good, meaningful lives to the extent we try to be like Him. This is the key.

The Crux of Life

With all these promises of peace and happiness, we still must cope with fear and anxiety. How will I pay the bills? will she go out with me again? can we save our marriage? how did I do on the test? what will happen with my business? will the car make it to Maine? how am I going to do in my new job? why does my child have this disease? why is the world in such a mess? what's going to happen in the future?

Everyone is confronted with the uncertainty and perplexity of life. However, at the same time we experience spiritual longings and leadings. Our individual and collective response to this tension is the great saga of evolution: How do we deal with it? This is the balance and interchange between the inner and outer worlds, our inner experience and life around us.

No matter what our status or phase of life, we must confront the real fear and anxiety which can press in and many times overwhelm and destroy. Most people struggle with these daily concerns and are the unrecognized heros who cook meals, mow lawns, tuck in covers, read stories, clean toilets, protect our cities, and give hugs. Human beings are equal in the struggle with uncertainty and in spiritual potential. God's given everyone the same spiritual raw material and opportunities.

Dealing with It
The desire for happiness in the face of uncertainty is the story of philosophy and the genesis for religion and spirituality. We recognize there is a better way, an alternative to unhappiness and anxiety. *Finding it is the crux of life.*

Most of us respond to uncertainty with fear and anxiety, like all animals do. We do this because of our animal inheritance. We seek to control the outside world to get rid of fear and anxiety. If we can control it, we'll know what's coming and get what we think we need to survive. Then we'll feel better. After all, we reason, it's all about animal survival. Our chief tools are blind optimism and blind pessimism.

Of course, we feel spiritual realities and also have a need to use these in life's problems. The challenge is to overcome selfishness, blind optimism, and blind pessimism with true spiritual assurance, a spiritual perspective. *Anything that impairs our spiritual experience is garbage: Our doubts, thoughts, attitudes, or confusion that block recognition of the truth are not part of the Universal Religion.*

Spiritual Assurance

When we spend time with God and accept what He gives, we're bathed in total spiritual assurance and certainty: We're guaranteed we'll make it and thrive to live eternal life and get everything we'll need when we need it. We accept the fact that the best life we could imagine is nothing compared to what God craves for us. It's nothing compared to God's will. We just need to do it with faith: Respond to the unseen.

If we embrace the most intense experience of all, God, we realize we're privileged to be here (whatever circumstance we're in) to grow and do God's will. All life's challenges begin to produce joy and spiritual confidence. We know they're the raw materials we need to grow. We have spiritual certainty in the face of material uncertainty. We welcome it. We thrive on it.

We recognize that none of the qualities we admire in others would be possible but for this struggle with uncertainty, fear, anxiety, and doubt. Our main battle is with doubt. If we stop doubting the spiritual experience that's more intense than the sun, we'll wake up. The amount of time we spend with God in prayer, service, contemplation, play, etc., is the amount of time we're happy. The portion of your life that you feel and live with God, is the portion that's real and joyful.

Consequently, we're freed from the fear of physical death and limitations, intellectual confusion, selfishness, incompleteness, limited thinking, time, and all human imperfection. *Any personal character problem can be solved. You become spiritually invincible.*

In the final analysis, the very things we fear and lament are the things that can help us become more like God. Without these challenges we never know spiritual joy or happiness. It's been said that the greatest affliction is to never have been afflicted.

Spiritual experience is so real, it's undeniable. We've got no right to deny it, to deny life.

Embarking for Happiness

Before you stands a fact, your sonship with God, your divine birthright that nothing can steal from you, no organization, person, action, or thought. How dare anyone try to be the controller or dealer of our spiritual status with God!

It's inconceivable that anything that's happened, is happening, or will happen, can interfere with your relationship with God if you really want to participate. This fact of sonship may be unbelievable to our old thinking, or the envious, but it's our right in the Universal Religion.

I invite you to trust your heart and act on what it says and be determined and steadfast to know the truth of life. Before you awaits an entire universe filled with joy, mystery, adventure, effort, gutsy decisions, relationships of value, and endless progress in the supreme satisfaction of knowing God and serving others.

How many times have we admired the soldier, the reformer, or the person who realizes her dreams? This hour is yours to sculpt your future and join the artistry of God's family. Imbibe in the noble pursuit of God and all things of joy and merit, of greatness. This is your right, a fact, for you are a child of God.

If you're unhappy, dissatisfied with life and the way it's been going, tired of feelings of frustration, confusion, helplessness, fear, anxiety, and loneliness, if you feel part of a meaningless world as a meaningless person, think you're a failure or an outcast from your family or friends, or lack self-confidence, power, motivation, or a sense of purpose, the spiritual breezes await your faithful springing jump. If you don't know what to do next, long for life to be more exciting and magical, more wondrous and fulfilling (and even if you have a great deal of pride and success) I invite you to experience sonship with God and discover the full possibilities of a spiritual life.

Your old decaying living will metamorphose as God changes you and helps meet the impossible problem. He does this, not because you belong to a certain group, or have a certain status, or have done certain deeds, but because He **loves** you, His little child. I invite you to boldly grip the hand of the Infinite with courage and trust as a little child.

You've probably heard most of this before. But, if you aren't excited, intrigued, and invigorated with burning hope and anticipation, I entreat you: Drink from the spiritual reservoir within. Only with faith, only by taking risks with God can you know the real meaning of peace, assurance, and spiritual growth. Risk. Find all! This is it!

If I told you there was a flood coming, what would you do? If I said a friend was critically injured in a car accident, how would you act? If your doctor said you had cancer, how would you feel? Most of us would pay attention and do something. But how do most of us react when we're told we're the children of God?

It's time we base our lives on faith and courage instead of fear and apprehension! We should believe in the joyful things, not just the painful or threatening events. The truths in this book can be experienced. Some say they cannot or that we need substitutes for God. Others will tell you what to think, decide, and do. Let's learn to search for ourselves and stop sabotaging our lives. Let's get rid of the garbage!

You're standing, an explorer before a magnificent journey into an unknown region, animals ready with provisions and equipment. You're prepared and have the necessary items. While your map shows where you are, you're about to leave it; you're at the beginning, distancing yourself from the surety and easy ways of tradition and acceptance. The day is bright. The rising plain of grass extends out, an undulating ocean in the swift, stimulating breeze. The brown, red, and gray expanse gives way to distant shapes touching the sky. You know this is your quest, to discover what lies beyond these plains and even the distant forms. All preparations made, you're as ready as you can be. It's time to act, to leave for the palate of new experiences and wonders.

> *The day shall not be up so soon as I,*
> *To try the fair adventure of tomorrow.*
>
> Shakespeare, from *King John III*

For one moment, forget the doubts, fears, and the intellectual arguments, and trust yourself, your ability to know the truth and be right. If your life isn't working or satisfying, then only by admitting this will you find more. Only by listening will you know and experience. Just listen to your heart and say, "I am ready . . ."

Spiritual Truths

Happiness and an eternal
destiny can be yours.

You are a child of a
perfect Father-God.

God can save you from
all limitations of self.

If you sincerely try,
you will experience God.

Your inner experience of God is firsthand
and independent of others.

If you desire God wholeheartedly,
nothing can get between you and God.

Our Loving Father

A Person, a Friend
Chapter 2

O

We've started a journey; we've dug up the secrets of true spirituality to see our destination. With these accomplishments it's time to move toward real satisfaction and saturating peace. A continuing successful voyage requires an understanding of our Creator since His personality and our conception of Him have a pervasive affect on our lives and what we can expect in the universe.

God's Name
To describe our Creator, we use a variety of changing words, usually analogies to admirable human behavior. We do this because it's easier to describe God with familiar and meaningful words—our terms. As each of us selects a name for God, our names should reflect His role and attitude toward us. This is extremely useful and ultimately inescapable since spiritual advancement requires that we quench our curiosity about God.

For us to know our Creator, our name for God must be *personal* and show the greatest human qualities while including gender, although God is genderless. While some feel otherwise, I stress that God is more personal if we use gender. Attempting to refer to God without gender would rob us of full identification with Him since we've got to identify with a person and all people in our experience have gender. A genderless person is beyond our experience and imagination. God's name must have gender so we may emulate Him and open the gates of our minds.

The Blind Child

I know what mother's face is like,
*   Although I cannot see;*
It's like the music of a bell;
*   It's like the roses I can smell—*
Yes, these it's like to me.

I know what father's face is like;
*   I'm sure I know it all;*
It's like his whistle on the air;
*   It's like his arms which take such care*
And never let me fall.

And I can tell what God is like—
*   The God whom no one sees.*
He's everything my parents seem;
*   He's fairer than my fondest dream,*
And greater than all these.

Anonymous

Keeping this in mind, I'll refer to God as the Universal Father, or Father, since He takes on the role of family head, protector, and primary supporter. While not all fathers take this place, and also due to the fact that both parents are increasingly required and choose to perform both parental roles, most fathers *have* functioned traditionally through history. Consequently, this image is woven with our ideals of human family relationships. Of course, mothers are *equal* to fathers, but they have historically taken different roles as loving parents.

When we use the name "Father" it helps to remember and respect the invaluable strength mothers give to families: Women are the matchless foundations for successful families. Nevertheless, because of God's role as initiator, upholder, and protector, the ideal and only way to understand Him is as Father. But, it's up to you; you must choose a word that best describes God and reflects His role.

A mother thinks of it this way:

> It doesn't have a gender quality to me, the word "father" when I'm talking about God . . . And it's not about an authority figure either. To tell you the truth, I think sometimes that it doesn't bother me because it has this feeling of a very large love. Mother love is something that you sort of expect. When a father loves you it just seems bigger. I can't quite explain it . . .
>
> . . . the sense of a fatherly love, it's so huge, it's so big, it encompasses great deals of acceptance. And I know a lot of people would like to use the word "father-mother" God, and that's fine . . . I just don't think of God as a gender. It's real hard to think of God as an old man, the old wise man kind of thing. I think of God as so replete that to limit God to a gender is kind of ridiculous. And yet the word "father" . . . we don't have a word in English that takes care of it. That's pretty much what the problem is. We don't have that word for parent that is all-encompassing. And we don't have many parents that are models that we could say "well, that's a parent', that's what a parent is." Until something better comes along, it works for me —Father.

A father had these thoughts . . .

> A lot of people when they think of God as father use the parallel of their earthly parents, they see God in that role . . . but I take it to mean that we are to understand the way God relates to us the way we relate to our children. I have a much better insight into God as father *as* a father, than I do as a child . . . I know that if my children are in trouble, I will do anything to help them—

that's an incredible bond, an incredible devotion to them; the parent will literally do *anything* for the child.

The child doesn't understand that very much, but the parent knows . . . I as a father know what I would do for my children, and so when I relate to God in that way I'm not relating as imagining myself as the child and God as the father, but looking at it from God's eyes . . . and then all the questions about forgiveness or compassion or judgment are right in their position. A child can misunderstand the parent and thoughts about forgiveness or judgment or sternness or any of those other things. But as a parent I understand exactly what that's all about. I always remind myself about that particular thing. That really makes a big difference in this concept of the father.

So, everyone is struck with the fact that they must find a name for God, the God *they* know daily. It's this experience of God that provides a unity for humankind while giving rise to the urge to know, imitate, and understand Him. With this need, let's make our *own* decisions and move to other considerations about God and how to understand Him.

God is a Real Person

It's astonishing: The initial foundations of a thing, entity, process or person determine what follows under any circumstances in any time and place for any duration. Take a garden. If the soil and location is right, and the proper combination of plants are woven together, protected, and nourished, we can expect a comforting natural architecture of soothing fragrances, brilliant colors, and pleasant places to rest.

Our lives mirror gardens, but it's imperative we understand God to find what we need. *Our principles and beliefs determine our level of happiness and quality of life.* All too often many don't live consciously. Instead they neglect the essentials of happiness and joy which is an understanding of

God. There can be no higher priority than laying the careful, stable, fulfilling foundations of a great and noble life. We should remember that it's only possible with God, a person.

To continue our understanding of God, we'll have to use metaphors and analogies. While they're necessary, we can't take them literally. Albeit we're of origin in God, He isn't a reflection of us, His imperfect creatures. Our Father is the wellspring of all, and is true, beautiful, and good in infinite ways, most being incomprehensible and unimaginable. God is our perfect parent and shouldn't be understood as representing human qualities. God is the only perfect *and* unlimited being, nothing less.

Like this person though, we've got misconceptions about God that need to be pruned off the spiritual tree:

> I think the principle misconception I had was that God was not a loving God, but was a God of wrath, vengeance, a lot of that, and also didn't have much fun. I think God has fun, as well as all the other things that He has. And the God that I grew up with didn't have any fun. He was very serious . . . stern.

Another person had this to say . . .

> The biggest misconception about God is that God wants for me something I wouldn't want for me, the idea that doing God's will is something odious and not really something I'd want to do; It's not good for me; my life is gonna be the pits; I've gotta serve time in Ethiopia or something like that.
>
> And just coming at it and realizing God isn't a task master, He's not mean, He's not this, He's not stern, and all those things, He's a parent who wants for His children, even in this life, the *best* that can happen. It doesn't mean easy; I don't want my kids to have a life that's a bed of marshmallows; I know that's not good for them. But nor do I want them to have a terrible tough life. That's not the issue. I know that their lives are gonna be relatively tough. It's the realization that what I want for

them is so much more than what they can possibly
conceive, like God and me.

It's true we've got to be careful comparing God to
ourselves, but the most important parallel we have is self-
consciousness. We know that we know; we know we *are*
somebody, a distinct part of the world. When we look at the
sea and find waves lapping up and the shapes of ships
moving in the distance, we know we're neither. When a child
says "I," she's saying that the "I" is speaking. When we
recognize we aren't part of a table, a tree, or the sky, we
know where we are and that we *know* it and can see we're
unique. Undoubtedly, God does this and gives this ability of
abilities, and potential of potentials. God knows He exists
and recognizes Himself as distinct from His universe creation.

Furthermore, we know ourselves because we recognize
ourselves; there is no one or no thing that's like you. Just as
people are unique, God is unique, not only as a person, but
as the source of all others; He shares His ability to know
Himself so we may know ourselves, the gift of self-
consciousness. It's only because we're unique that we're
allowed to distinguish ourselves from the world.

Just as we recognize ourselves, we can see personality in
others, God included. Only a person can look at a body and
know it's animated by another, and then share ideas and
actions with this other for meaning. Relationships are
between *people* in the process of knowing they know each
other and that they're growing together. No doubt these
things are possible with God since He's a person. He knows
us and our location, and is always able to recognize us. Likewise, if we're sensitive, we're always able to appreciate and
acknowledge Him where He reveals himself. **We can get to
know God**.

The importance of our God-relationship is revealed in this interview:

> As I know God, it's a relationship rather than a person in the sense that a relationship is something you enter into and with; it's not isolated or apart. And you have that ability to become one with another in a relationship. God as person to me . . . becomes friend, becomes confidant, becomes someone I revive into my life and receptive to and giving to at the same time. I realize I have the ability to become one with, enter into fullness with that person without separation. I don't enter into judgment with that relationship.
>
> What's more, I feel I have the ability to have that relationship with God's children, a relationship I can enter into and become one with another human being, and I cannot be separate from, not be in judgment of. And I'm taught that through the actual experience of God in my life.
>
> Not having God would be somewhat like walking around without my head on or walking around without my heart in my body, that I would be walking around without feelings and thoughts, walking around without a dimension that made me more than a slug. I feel that relationship defines me, it enhances me, it grows me, it's productive in my life; it's constantly expanding me as a human being. So without it I would remain stagnant, undefined . . . maybe I would be more defined, but in a lesser way . . . I certainly feel like I would have no reason to move, to grow, to learn.
>
> There is this sense that the fabric of our being is God, and from that we grow out; it's our seed, our spiritual seed; and we grow from that. If you didn't have that seed, what would you grow? Why would you grow? You would have no reason to. So it's constantly regenerating because of our spirit kernel, which to me is our God essence.

People know each other and God through *communication*, usually speaking their thoughts, although there are many

methods. Can the Father communicate to others? Think about
how powerful and eternal He is . . . Is it really possible? Be
assured God uses many techniques of communication since
He's a person yearning to know others. God knows our
thoughts and communicates with us when we make it
possible. It's true this communication is somewhat limited
(Let's remember the baby at the beginning of the first
chapter.), but it's real since there are two people here: God
and you.

> *Knowledge of revelation does not always begin with
> clarity. It may increase in clarity; it should do so. It may,
> however, diminish also in clarity. But under all circum-
> stances, it begins with certitude . . . Doubt and despair,
> human unbelief, and even a sea of uncertainties on our
> part, will not be able to change the certitude of His
> presence.*
>
> Karl Barth

Communication with God is possible. From this we can
assume God has thoughts (This is the best word we can use.)
just as we use thoughts to represent the world. People are
aware of their surroundings by visualizations; people see
pictures along with feelings and experience values *felt* and
known. It's crude to say the Creator thinks like us, but it
wouldn't be wrong to say God is able to "think" about things.

The result of this thinking process is a decision-action.
God and people carry out their plans (Everything you do is
based on a decision you have just made or the affects of
many decisions you made before.); everyone is responsible
for his of her actions. Only a person can think, plan, visualize, and feel to determine his or her destiny. If we think
about them *first*, our actions are decisions, not merely
reactions but proactive behavior independent of the environment. Our Father has this potential in the ultimate sense; for
His decisions are eternal and cannot be described as ever

happened; they always were; they simply **are**. They are independent of time and space.

And in our discussion, how can we forget our sensing abilities? What would life be like without senses, windows to the world? Clearly, our God has His methods of sensing, unlimited ways to know the universe which He designs and creates. While we have physical senses and other ways of knowing, God's techniques are limitless and breathtaking, embracing different types of beings and angels, and of course, us. Nonetheless, He doesn't need them, or us, but kindly gives everyone the pleasure of participating with Him.

Therefore, God has relationships much as we do by communicating ideas and interacting with others. A relationship with God is for the sake of a common goal and for the benefit of others (as in other relationships). To know God is to have the most gratifying relationship possible, one laced with mutual appreciation and loyalty.

God-consciousness is pleasant and attains deeper, a more intense communication level than human relationships can. The devotion and happiness you've known in past partnerships are a starting point with God. He wants to have an eternal union with you and is ready! I think God created the universe to know and be known, to love and be loved because these delightful celebrations are ends in themselves. God has them just as we do.

With these characteristics of God in mind, it's time to look at how He relates to His creation.

What is energy, power, or matter? Is God this physical stuff? When I look far out at the vast swirling galaxies of light and energy, I'm amazed at their scope and power. When I see a volcano rush out streams of fresh hot rock and fierce winds or gentle waterways travel over to expanses of oceans, human works pale and I feel great humility.

Our ancestors had these feelings. But, is this God? Do we look inside a flower to find the Infinite Upholder, or a sunset, or listen to bird echo? Does God personify nature's wonders and the universe? Is God the laws of physics or the revelations of geology?

From what we know about God, the answer is "No." It's helpful to remember God is a person in every sense with the accompanying abilities and characteristics, but when we try to shove God in the tiny box of mere physics or natural beauty, we're doing what our forbearers did for millennia. It was natural for man to see nature as an all-powerful group of people or person that controlled life. Let's not regress into this misconception since God is not a collection of physical elements, a derivation of nature, or its result.

The Universal Father is the Creator and originator, the *source* of reality. Every particle of physical matter, the immeasurable celestial stretches and life on earth, come from God but are not Him. The Father created matter as our habitat by designing and establishing physical laws. God is not nature, but nature is from God.

> The one God, the first and sole and universal Maker and Lord, had nothing coeval with him, not infinite chaos, not measureless water, or solid earth, or dense air, or warm fire, or subtle breath, nor the azure cope of the vast heaven: but He was one, alone by Himself, and by His will He made the things that are, that before were not, except so far as they existed in His foreknowledge.
>
> Hippolytus, third century

Before the universe, before the first gas cloud exploded with stars and the first water drop, the eternal Father made a plan to create matter. As we appreciate the pleasing design of a building, or the creamy strokes of a painter, when we enjoy fine food or are soothed in song, we know a person is behind them. Similarly, God designed the universe: The painting doesn't create the painter; the house doesn't produce the architect or builder; only a person can give birth to another and create beauty. Only a perfect Creator could unfold the delicate and powerful celestial tapestry we touch.

To look at matter and say God is similar is foolhardy. The Creator is not a consciousness made of the universe since He doesn't gain power or personality from it. He's its *source*. Matter is a tool for God in the execution of His mandates and goals. He isn't "Silly Putty" to be molded and manipulated as needed but is a changeless and profoundly stable friend. God isn't limited or even described by physics since it's His tool for things, not a style of relating to people as some believe.

In addition to God's primacy, He is immeasurable. Although we define objects with instruments, God is beyond their reach and further advancements as much as fine music is beyond a single-celled organism. God is a person known only through a living relationship and this friendship is through the soul, not the senses, not physical stuff. We admire the great universe, but to know God, we have to live the days with Him.

These conclusions follow this fact: **God is a Person!!!** Being able to know and be known, to do all things people can, God gives life a new dynamism and meaning, a goal to reach for. Our lives would profoundly change if we didn't understand God is a person, if we thought God anything less. *Your decisions and actions are determined and molded by your conception of God or the absence of a belief in God as a person.*

Imitating God

We are strivers by nature. Everyone has a conscious or unconscious goal, an undeniable and inexorable longing to develop and become complete. Despite the fact that many abandon this perfection urge (either for selfishness, apathy, or fear), most people base their activities and reactions on this goal *with the intent of becoming like their idea of perfec-*

tion. Human beings live to transform themselves, to imitate the source of their existence, that which they think is perfect. Human change is the process of imitation, copying, mirroring, and patterning: We change when we imitate. Virtually everyone moves through life straining to grow to attain some vision of perfection, consciously or not.

Children seek to become like their parents. They observe them dressing, see them coping with pain and experiencing joy, and are fascinated with their use of language. There is no end to their imitation and, incidentally, nothing wrong with this growth act, this human instinct. Unfortunately, many *choose* to end the imitation of heros and the use of ideals, values, and principles and instead lead poisonous lives of festering egotism or indifference—unconsciousness, death.

It's critical we learn to transfer parental imitation to our Creator. As we find God's ways and will, our ideal of a perfect person should change because He's our new priority, our consummate role model and standard for all sincerity, thought, and conduct.

Unfortunately, countless people cease to look for a hero or heroine at the age when they should seek out and imitate their divine parent. The child in them has forgotten. When they assume God contains the negative aspects of their parents, doesn't exist, or is unimportant, they're using a primitive defense mechanism—denial. They become prejudiced and fearful and tragically lose trust and faith, the faith of a little child, and consequently devalue their experience of God, the very person they crave but deny. These people have no role model and are drowning minute by minute in a toxic sea of uncertain anxiety.

Since the longing for growth-happiness remains, this need for role models is filled by people or things. Many substitute human leaders for God, simultaneously denying His existence and enthusiastically copying their new leader, while others believe the universe is governed by an intelligent energy and inevitably fixate on becoming like this energy. They feel they've grown when they have more power to manipulate the world for their desires or to avoid a problem.

The thrills and accomplishments of life are reduced to satisfying selfish desires and avoiding real growth. Finally, there is only bitter anger, depression, and disappointment, resentment for the world that won't change at a whim. *If we try to become like anything but God, we become like anything but God and feel the pain, the marked tragedy of deserting our destiny.* The harvest of life becomes diseased and dead without the Universe Maker as role model.

Let's listen to this person's experience:

> When I get off balance I become very self-centered. I got way way off balance about seven or eight years ago and thought I could do it all myself and I didn't really need to relate to an organized religion or a Jesus or something like that. And so I struck out and went through some craziness like going through a divorce. And everything really began to cascade downward.
>
> And so I've been coming back up out of that in terms of some sort of a transformation. And so that's why I'm feeling comfortable now that I can step off this crazy treadmill and go do what I'm supposed to do rather than doing what is the popular impressions of what I should be doing.
>
> The impressions that society, and family and people, would put on me, O.K. you've got the potential to go and achieve all this stuff, go do that cause that's your mission in life. Having gotten to that point (I basically achieved everything I set out to achieve from a material standpoint.) I can now sit back and say "O.K., I can go now and do what I'm supposed to be doing." Maybe if I had had a stronger connection with God I would have been able to get to this sooner rather than playing out a role . . .
>
> . . . And I see so many other people playing out this role without a good spiritual connection. And indeed, if

> you don't have a spiritual connection, I don't think you
> have any choice in this life but just to play out the roles
> . . . It's like saying "Alright, I've been dealt a hand of
> cards and I have to play out that hand." In reality, you
> can turn that set of cards in and get another deck if you
> have a spiritual connection.

Dead-end lives and unchanging dissatisfactions arise from a lack of understanding God and neglecting the effort to become like Him. Ultimately, this usually brings us to Him.

The human urge to imitate requires answering a few fundamental questions: Who am I? What am I supposed to be doing? How do I do it? Where am I going? Sooner or later, each person must answer these questions by understanding God because viable answers come no other way. We are children of God by definition; to be human and alive is to know you are a child of God and strive to do His will.

If I were a flower, I would've started from a seed that's dependent on soil, water, sun and air, and would look about similar to other flowers of my seed type. As this plant I would be unable to know I existed or to communicate with others; I would be devoid of personal characteristics. At death, my life would end since flowers simply don't have many abilities or possibilities. To use biologic laws to describe a flower's origin and destiny is appropriate and true but a gross blunder applied to a person's life.

This sounds straightforward, but many of us don't realize the assumptions we've made about our purpose and destiny. If we view ourselves nothing more than products of evolution with short meaningless lives, then we've discarded our humanity for confused intellectual conclusions. If we believe there's no purpose to life and exercise only a desire to find pleasure and avoid pain, then this is all we'll do.

The nourishment of the soul, the illumination of the mind, and the invigoration of the heart is strictly found by embracing the Maker of the soul, mind, and heart. Materialistic fertilizer only contaminates the soil for spiritual growth and eventually destroys the material-driven human. Whereas the touch of the Universal Father assures the materialist of his place in eternity and frees him to form a philosophy of truth for doing good and creating beauty, transforming him into a *faith* child of God. Then this person transcends nature to make spiritual decisions independent of the environment instead of being its mere slave.

We are people and have self-consciousness from God for a reason. Our actions and the answers to our questions are seen through the lens of being a person. Our uniqueness defines us and is the secret of being human —*the ultimate gift from God.* Everything flows from this. To understand what to do as a person, we've got to look at happy people, people who live with God, and not to unfruitful individuals, a gas cloud in space, an earthquake, or an energy field as a role model.

This woman has a healthy and mature heroine:

> When I was in my early twenties I was married to a man who had a very wonderful family. His mother was very graceful, very gracious, very forgiving, always looking on the bright side of people . . . it's something that affected me so deeply that it's become a guiding inspiration later on.
>
> I was visiting my in-laws and I went out with some friends and got really drunk, and came back, and she was having a dinner party that night. I was the guest of honor; she was introducing me to some of her friends. I ended up passing out before anybody showed up because I had been out on the beach all day with my sister-in-law drinking.
>
> I just missed the whole dinner, obviously. Thank God I didn't come home when everybody showed up. So my mother-in-law had made all this effort, put this party on for me, and had to make excuses for me. And I woke up the next morning in horror thinking of this horrible

thing that I had done to my mother-in-law and how upset she would naturally be with me.

So I walked into the kitchen where she was sitting at the kitchen table doing her Bible study. And I started out by saying "I don't know what happened last night . . . " and she interrupted me and said "Well, I do. You just haven't been eating enough." . . . (If I had done that on a reoccuring basis it would be a dysfunctional response.), she recognized the fact that I was young and stupid, didn't know how to hold my liquor, and that it wasn't important to get some kind of justice out of what I had done to her dinner party. Instead, the important thing at that moment was to restore my self-respect.

I was so floored by the fact that she would have such a loving, caring response to me, and to absolve me from guilt and to try to reestablish my sense of self, that it made me want to be the person that she was acknowledging inside. And from that point on I realized how important it was to help people believe in themselves because of what she had done for me and what that felt like. I knew that that was something I wanted to do for other people.

Because our Father is a person, we can exist to experience the satisfactions, joys, and pleasures of life, and know we are experiencing them. By responding effectively to challenges, by living desires, drives, and lures the spiritual way, the personal way, we grow. It's these desires, drives, and lures that are the essential ingredients of a thrilling meaningful life, God's gifts enabling us to know Him and others. Our satisfactions, joys, and pleasures are the rewards, the carrots bringing happiness. This process of motivation and growth is only experienced and fulfilled because *we're people*. We couldn't exist as people if God weren't a person, the source of self-consciousness.

So, it's obvious that the most satisfying and meaningful experience is a healthy relationship. What would our lives be without people? Who could exist without friends with whom to share and help? Material things won't satisfy our longings, a person's longings, the soul's thirst. Yet we continually see people trying the impossible; they avoid others and expect to be happy without them—amazing. When all is said and done, the association of two people in friendship is the central quest, the most precious stone. Nothing else comes close.

All this is only possible because God is a person who creates people. No other kind of God or presence could suffice. The basic lesson in life is the sincere imitation of God, the first person, to become the best person you can. We don't grow or satisfy ourselves by mimicking non-personal things or selfish people, but by emulating selfless serving friends, family, and acquaintances.

> *When Jesus talked about "the living God," he referred to a personal Deity — the Father in heaven. The concept of the personality of Deity facilitates fellowship; it favors intelligent worship; it promotes refreshing trustfulness. Interactions can be had between non-personal things, but not fellowship. The fellowship relation of father and son, as between God and man, cannot be enjoyed unless both are persons. Only personalities can commune with each other . . .*
>
> *The Urantia Book*

It then becomes blatantly clear that we conduct life based on whether we believe God is a person or an energy. Our behavior is the question. How should we treat others and run our affairs with them? The answer is based on our values and principles, of which there can be two types, personal and non-personal, the emulation of selfless people or just the mimicking of things.

If you're trying to become more like God the person, you'll strive to be the best person you can and identify with the positive and progressive people around you, taking joy in serving them, having relationships with them. By striving for ideal relationships you'll become a better friend and be wrapped in a protective blanket of other true friends. These healthy friendships will thrive because you'll have satisfied your *imitation need* for perfection with absolute perfection; you'll know God.

The more we believe God to be a non-person, the more we'll believe others and ourselves as non-persons. If we see them as objects, merely physical creatures, we'll disregard their needs as people and mistreat them. Moreover, we'll fail to see them in the right perspective as well-meaning children of God who can have an eternal career, creatures seeking growth, doing their best. This ability to empathize, to see people as people and try to understand them, is true conduct —the compassion of personality-self-consciousness.

In addition to hurting others, the more we're puppets of selfish urges and threatening events, the more of ourselves we'll deaden, the more of ourselves we'll put to sleep. Each purely selfish thought diminishes our experience and ourselves, a subtle mutilation of our souls and a dimming of our light of life. By becoming increasingly subject to physical urges and selfish desires, we become more controlled, totally subject to physical laws like rocks, trees, and animals. We eventually slip out of humanity.

The kernel of human life is transcendence of the environment by freedom of self-consciousness, memory, forethought, moral decisions, and spiritual experience. We know what's going on but only know that we are because we can recognize and care for others. Self-consciousness is nurtured by having relationships with others—other-consciousness.

To be human is to know you exist, not only for your benefit *but for that of others.* To be human is to know your origin is nature but your destiny is God. You know your eternal life is independent but respectful of nature. While the body is temporary, a human being knows the core of human life is a connection with God, the promise of life eternal. The clearest definition of humanity, then, is the process of spiritual growth from humble elements to divine shores.

Ultimately, nothing would be possible but for the astounding fact that God is a person who created us as people; we are in His image. Our lives are filled with ambitions and rewards and the ability to know ourselves and others. By learning about ourselves and others the right way, our ambitions and goals become noble and valuable. We must touch each other selflessly to achieve these noble goals. When we're together, we benefit by benefitting each other. Truly, of all experiences that are valued, the association of two people is the highest. Friendship is best! And our ultimate friendship is with God.

God is a person.

Spiritual Truths

God is a perfect person.

God has all the abilities that people do.

God is the source of everything
and everybody.

Our goal is to imitate God.

The Nature of God

What God is Like
Chapter 3

O

Alright, we say God is a viable and thriving person, but this is insufficient since there are many varieties of persons. God's nature determines the potential of our relationship with Him and directs its techniques. How does He behave and feel toward us? What are His expectations for our lives and what can we expect from Him? Will He crack the whip of reality as a taskmaster or feed us luscious spiritual candies, or be somewhere in the middle?

It's important we dig to examine these momentous questions because their answers determine our approaches to life and our personal growth rates. Although some of this chapter may seem childish, simple, or obvious, our happiness depends on *childlike acceptance* of these fundamental understandings about God as much as physics and chemistry is supported by knowing addition and subtraction.

God's Perfection
Before we get too far, it's vital to understand that God is absolutely perfect and changeless, complete as He is. This doesn't mean God is crystalline and removed from His

universe or children, but rather His personality and actions, His plan, won't change and hasn't ever changed.

It's natural that people change constantly, but you may rely on God to stay the same, stable and reliable, rather than be someone you can manipulate or coerce, flatter, convince, or placate. God is utterly, undeniably changeless in His person and is our buttress, our foundation forever.

> *Almost everything said of God is unworthy, for the very reason that it is capable of being said.*
>
> St. Gregory the Great

Therefore, we shouldn't expect or ask God to alter His plan for our temporary gratification or kicks (which is often our first reaction). Adversity and poignant problems are designed to put stress on us and should lead us to change *ourselves* rather than whine and whimper. Ideally we engage in a partnership with God activated by a complete desire to change for the benefit of others, ourselves, and God. When we encounter depression, fear, and anxiety, we can use these feelings to wake us up to invigorating spiritual exertion, instead of quitting.

Asking God to change is shortsighted, lazy, and immature. We misunderstand the privilege of personal change and find only depression, misunderstanding, and frustration. To know God is changeless is to know complete peace and confidence in our divine parent as we course through the multitude of personal and environmental variations and all the ups and downs of life. To know God is constant is a relief!

This is how one person felt about this truth:

> I think to know that God is changeless is very securing because His attitude towards me and everyone is always the same and infinitely perfect. It gives you a feeling of comfort. And as you grow to know that

attitude and know that personality more and more, you just grow to love it more. It gives you a real sense of security.

I'm not totally, always, questioning "Am I doing God's will?" or "Am I not doing God's will?" because my purpose is to do God's will and I'm only human. I know that His attitude towards me is gonna be the same whether I do it right or whether I do it wrong . . . I don't believe that God's a wrathful God who all of a sudden has a whim and hates me one day and loves me the next because I do this or do that.

Certainly God is changeless because He's perfect. As we continue trying to understand God, we must always think of Him as **perfect**, perfection personified, the universe pattern of personal perfection. He transcends our vision of perfection and has no flaw. Certainly, humans are a jumble of good and bad, but the Creator has no problem, annoyance, or deficit because He's the pattern and ideal of how we're to live; He's our model.

God's Helpfulness

Just as we enjoy helping others, so does God. To aid a friend, to help a stranger find her way in a new city or help a child learn to read is kindness. At every avenue there's an opening to perform some distinct gentle assistance to illuminate someone's life, perhaps for more than a day. And as we gain pleasure and joy from service, so does God.

God delights in touching us with an infinite caress as a parent loves a child. The Maker of humankind knows us thoroughly and is in the best position to be kind to us, to help us with understanding and respect. The act of God freeing us to solve problems on a daily, even second-by-second basis, is the great *comfort* of life.

Frequently it's hard to help a friend in need, even though we may drain ourselves in the effort. To spend an hour or so with a friend is a great service and exercises purpose and loyalty. But we have limits. While we give all to a friend in distress, our time is extremely restricted since there are many other things we must do. After a while, a disturbed friend who isn't getting better may become a burden and a frustration. Often we think we can't help, but the Father has no such constraints.

Instant by instant God awaits your listening ear regardless of anything you've done, are doing, or will do (God knows the future.). If you think of the most insurmountable problem you agonize over, if you dredge and drag out your most despised flaws, it will have no effect on God's attitude. This will, nonetheless, prepare you to recognize God's love and stupendous affection if you're *sincere and wholehearted.* Just think. God is always here with an embrace despite your moods and actions or self-concept!

> *O Lord, how entirely needful is thy grace for me, to begin any good work, to go on with it, and to accomplish it.*
> *For without that grace I can do nothing, but in thee I can do all things, when thy grace doth strengthen me.*
>
> Thomas à Kempis

Don't expect God to give help as an average human being would for He really will stop at nothing to assist in the truest sense: We receive what we need in the way we need it for as long as we need it, and at the right time. God has an *unlimited* reserve, a reservoir of love and support craving to touch you and be interwoven with your marrow. Whatever it takes, the Creator will surely give us what's within our capacity as long as we need it because His love is endless and unrestricted. In every situation, in every moment, help is not only on the way, but was there before we realized we needed it. Our loving Creator never discounts us and continuously strives to fill our celestial longings.

Here are two more examples:

> God helps me by making me aware of value in that situation. I know that even though it would be easier for me to yell at my kids and tell them to shut up and leave me alone, instead, because I know that value is there, I look at that value and see how I can respond to that situation. For example, I may be doing something that my kids don't like or makes them feel unsure. When they start whining at me to clamor for attention, instead of me doing the easy way out and telling them to leave me alone, I might say to myself "What's the truth in this situation?" And when I see the truth of the situation, when I avail myself of value in the situation, I can say "The truth in this situation is that these children need to be assured in this moment." I'm going to stop telling them to shut up and leave me alone and I'm going to see how we can address the problem that's here.
>
> I wouldn't normally do that if I didn't know that God was helping me seek value.

> The way that God helps me the most is by bringing friends into my life, by bringing His other personalities in to help me, to nurture me, to guide me, to love me. He helps me by bringing personalities and relationships into my life by sharing with me His love and His fullness of life and His understandings, through other people. By allowing me to recognize His presence in others is probably the greatest way that He helps me, by allowing me to love and be loved by other people, to respect and be respected by other people whom I also recognize as God-conscious, God-loving people.

Furthermore, the Creator couldn't be this helpful unless He truly understood all our human propensities. God knows *everything* about us (He created us.), our world, and our true desires even though our actions can indicate otherwise. We shouldn't be afraid that God will judge us for things we never meant to think, feel, or do, or those we fail to do. The Universal Father of spiritual evolution wouldn't reject us for simply experiencing part of the very growth he designed into us. Anyway, even if we mean to harm, God always wants us back in the family. God knows when we're sincere and realizes we loose control occasionally and even intentionally go wrong.

Sometimes we make terrible miscalculations and mistakes that cause others great pain or we keep behaving the same, every day, though we know there's another option. While our friends and family can doubt our sincerity despite our attempts to convince them, God knows us, where we want to go, and who we want to be. Our intentions and desires become clear. The real beauty is that God gives us just what we need at the right time. No one else is this understanding.

God is Eternal

Time. Time drifts away and we want things immediately— yesterday, instantaneous gratification. However, God is concerned only with real progress, not the time it takes to achieve. Since we're largely immature, we want sudden results and accelerated development in ourselves and the world in order to get what we want; we shun challenge and want to avoid difficult situations and painful circumstances to find only good times.

Think back to grade school when asking the teacher if it was recess yet, or in later years, awaiting word for a job? Who can forget waiting for a flight or a contract? Our lives burst with moments when we wish for things to happen immediately, frequently wanting results without the evolution and hard work that precedes them. Could God be anything like this? Does God want us to move along fast?

God knows how long and slow our maturation is. The Creator gains great satisfaction gazing at us as we slowly and persistently triumph over problems and great obstacles. Before and at each decision-juncture God provides help as part of His plan for you within His overall eternity-plan. No matter how many times you make the same silly mistake or commit a real wrong, your eternal parent is right there patiently setting you straight. Even though it may take an entire lifetime on earth to begin to understand a pesky old problem, it doesn't matter to God because your *progress* is important, not your rate of development.

The joy of life is in relishing daily living, intensely living so that time flies by and you taste eternal timelessness. To do this, we must not, again, be concerned with our speed: Understand that God doesn't tire or get bored with you. God goes at your pace and meets your needs with His love through the midst of repeated mistakes and rejections until finally you grow.

To God there's no time. God has always existed and so, His patience is infinite and thus, incomprehensible. Envision a great piece of granite, perched on a majestic peak in the high mountains. Daily, the wind, sun, and other elements whittle this stubborn rock till it vanishes and crumbles to individual grains. One of these grains weaves slowly downhill and finally to a stream bed and from here journeys to valleys and plains until brought to the ocean. While the time here is excruciatingly long and unimaginable, this event of geology is almost instantaneous for our Father who lives beyond time in eternity.

> *The created world is but a small parenthesis in eternity.*
>
> Sir Thomas Browne

> *I saw Eternity the other night,*
> *Like a great ring of pure and endless light.*
>
> Henry Vaughan

> *Eternal life is beyond past, present, and future . . .*
>
> Paul Tillich

Surely the Father can be with you through your apparently long years and mind-consuming problems!

As we found before, the growth rate isn't important since God is concerned with whether you're growing. You may find yourself making the same agonizing mistakes, asking why. But God doesn't give up on you and, in fact, absolutely believes in your capacity for growth and continued happiness. Since God created you, He knew how long it would take and what you'd need to be guided through the midst of problems and decisions. There's *always* a kind and understanding friend that can wait (and has) for you to enter the light, even though it may require a lifetime.

These people know of God"s patience:

> I'm a very impatient person. I'm the kind of person who grew up watching T.V. when the Cowboy got injured and he was fixed the next day; I expect everything to happen immediately. I get an idea in my mind and I want it to be so, *quickly*.
>
> God has been very patient with me, patient with my impatience. I feel He definitely watches over my slow growth. Even though you wanta love people and you want to do the right thing, we all probably find ourselves reflecting on things that we do that "Gosh, I shouldn't have been that way." or "I should've handled it this way." "I should have been more loving." "I should have been more understanding." "I should have been more patient."
>
> I find that His patience with me is really encouraging in a way because I realize that even though I may make the same error over and over again, that He's still there to forgive me. He's still patient enough and forgiving enough to realize that my intent is to get better, my intent is to try and grow.

> There isn't anything that you do short of perfection that God isn't patient with. It's only when you recognize you're being impatient with yourself that you have to tune in to His patience. Patience is pretty circumscribed.

You have to think of it as true understanding transcends
patience. It isn't a question of patience; it's a question
of infinite love.

That's where His patience comes from; He understands what we're facing and is therefore not only
sympathetic but is willing to help us through it if we'll let
Him.

What an absolute relief! What a joy! Any predicament or
challenge facing us, in spite of its duration, can be sur-
mounted with the most magnificent being *cheering* us on
with every small change to tantalizing nobility and spiritual
fireworks. In the maze of our endless confusion or resistance,
God sees and understands why it takes time. God never
ceases touching you with absolute love so that you may feel
your kinship with all and His desire to know and live with
you. Be assured, God knows your real intentions and holds
your hand at every turn for all time.

God's Concern

God's actions say one thing: He loves us and is interested in
everything we do. God's concerned with your every decision
and how it affects His relationship with you or the one He's
trying to begin. These things matter to God above all because
God values relationships above all.

What is the eternal significance of your actions? Does it
matter if you achieve great success in your field or job? Does
hairstyle hold value, or bathroom color, or car make? Some
concerns have value and ultimate meaning. Nevertheless, it's
a fact that many things we spend so much time enmeshed
with are insignificant to the spiritual work we should be
doing. All that matters to God is whether you're living in *the
spiritual way* that will bring yourself and others closer to
Him.

Your intentions, sincerity, willingness to act, and use of
faith are of prime concern to God. The Creator looks for

your desire to live the spiritual way and isn't judging you by any achievement. While friends and family may not show the concern you wish they would, God is with you and *cares* about every part of your life.

> The Lord is my shepherd; I shall not want.
> He maketh me to lie down in green pastures: He leadeth me beside the still waters.
> He restoreth my soul: He leadeth me in the paths of righteousness for his name's sake.
> Yea, though I walk through the valley of the shadow of death, I will fear no evil: For thou art with me; thy rod and thy staff they comfort me.
> Thou preparest a table before me in the presence of mine enemies: Thou anointest my head with oil; my cup runneth over.
> Surely goodness and mercy shall follow me all the days of my life: And I will dwell in the house of the Lord for ever.

23rd Psalm, The Bible

God is your constant companion and confidant. For example: When you're insulted God is trying to reveal the spiritual answer to the pain. When your child does splendidly in school, be comforted that God's concern has helped him. If you're in a relationship that's uncomfortable or superficial, your Father is awaiting the decision of you and your partner to listen to *Him*. Or when you're riding high on great satisfaction and accomplishment, God shares your joy but is concerned with continuing your spiritual growth. And of course, when you think it isn't worth trying, and are sinking into pain and despair, a gentle strong hand is reaching to pull you from those relentless waters. God wants to set you on the road of freedom and joy as a courageous child with the world as your ally.

Unlike most people we know of, God is completely sincere in His concern and interest. His purpose is to nurture you to know Him better and show others the way, since He cares for you with total, unwavering, intense love. You never have to doubt God's actions because He meets your needs whether you realize it or not, whether you acknowledge it or not. As you grow, you'll soon see that God is here and always ready to encourage and refresh your soul for difficulties and challenges.

You can trust God absolutely! Think of the many times people let you down or hurt you. Maybe it was a parent who abused you daily or a spouse who said he or she would work for a happy marriage, but left you stranded. Could it be a friend who used you for self-gain or pleasure? It may be an institution that gave you a slap in the face. But please remember, *this isn't God!*

God never hurts you or lets you down. It's hard to believe, even harder if people and events have driven us in the dirt like stakes, but if you stretch to find God with *total* effort you'll be touched by a person you couldn't have imagined, the one who transcends outside experience and every friendship.

These interviews reveal friendships with God:

> I talk to God all day long. I am constantly . . . all day I call Him dad, and pop. I treat Him as if He's my real father. I get along with Him better than I got along with my real father. I think it's wonderful. I have an ongoing relationship with God, daily, all day long . . .
> . . . I'm getting better at seeing God in other people which helps me to have a better relationship with Him through others . . . I think it's an extremely comforting position to be in.

> Human friends, you can't depend on them as much as you like. One of our problems in understanding the dynamics of friendship is that friends let you down, sometimes unintentionally. Sometimes they have a different agenda. Sometimes they're just insensitive to

what you need. But the Father always knows what you need, in every circumstance and in every situation.

I think that if you said "What single thing have you learned if you only learned one thing?" it would be that God is a friend. To me that was the ultimate truth, so to speak. So whatever happened to me (And a lot of things happened to me, and a lot of stuff to go through.) . . . once I got Him in the right place, once He was my friend, I think everything else fell into place. It's much, much easier now . . . It makes life meaningful now, where it didn't have any meaning before.

We tend to have misconceptions about God and forget His friendship because of bitter experiences with people. We can't know God by comparing Him to all people. Often we believe God is completely like our parents or that He brings unpleasant experiences as punishments. It's imperative we remember *we can understand God only by knowing Him as loving parent and true friend.* The only way to know God is to seek Him. Then you'll see God, a friend you can trust during any circumstance for as long as necessary. When you accept the reality of God, your illusions about Him will fade in truth-light and go to their rightful place in the cosmic landfill.

As you begin to trust God with faith you'll understand He *trusts* you. The Creator is confident His love will transfigure you to help others and know personal achievement. God trusts you'll use your gifts and His inspiration to artfully bring pleasure and hope to the everyday, invigorating yourself and the world. Even if you violate this trust, even if you misuse your talents, God will trust you again if you're sincere and hunger for the truth.

God's Truthfulness
Truth is everything in cosmic education and the hunger for it is a crucial component of spiritual progress and the

prerequisite of new understanding. No spiritual growth or satisfaction of knowing would be possible without a continual revelation of truth. Truth is the uniting glue illuminating experience, thought, intention, and action to form meanings, values, ideals, and principles.

When we ask God for the truth (examples of better patterns of living) it's given in the most helpful way. This doesn't mean God tells us all we want but that He tells us everything we *need* to know. He'll uncover truth that will aid us with problems at hand or the desire for more knowledge. Truth is like power and God gives us what we can understand, appreciate, and use. He wants the best for us.

Send Forth, O God, Thy Light and Truth

Send forth, O God, Thy light and truth,
And let them lead me still,
Undaunted, in the paths of right,
Up to Thy holy hill:
Then to Thy altar will I spring,
And in my God rejoice;
And praise shall tune the trembling string,
And gratitude my voice.

O why, my soul, art thou cast down?
Within me why distressed?
Thy hopes the God of grace shall crown;
He yet shall make thee blessed:
To Him, my never-failing Friend,
I bow, and kiss the rod;
To Him shall thanks and praise ascend,
My Saviour and my God.

John Quincy Adams

To find the truth is to gain an understanding of how to live the spiritual life and its meanings. Yes, there are scientific facts, but truth is flowing and redefined along with the *ways* we relate to one another. God perseveres to teach true spiritual living that helps everyone while revealing the most ideal service you can do for others.

As time goes on there will be new ways we can help each other and show consideration because they will be more effective than the old: The people we'll serve will have changing needs. True spiritual needs define service. In addition, our facts, meanings, and values will transmute to higher levels and reveal more truth.

The true way will change as we change because the most effective way to help someone yesterday may not be valid today. Achieving the greatest good for the greatest number for the longest time, as well as understanding God and our fellows, will require different techniques as our facts, meanings, and values refine. We'll know more and live in evolving patterns to enjoy life, to live with God who always shows us the way. Faith is the key to know spiritual stability and certainty during constant uncertain changes!

God's Righteousness

God set up and designed the universe for a purpose which none can say. But we do know in approaching this wonderful goal that God's rules, procedures, and consequences work together to achieve it. Creation is regulated by the Father's will in the areas of mind, matter, and spirit.

> *If one does not know the Constant, One runs blindly into disasters.*
>
> *If one knows the Constant, one can understand and embrace all.*
>
> *If one understands and embraces all, one is capable of doing justice.*
>
> *To be just is to be kingly; to be kingly is to be heavenly; to be heavenly is to be one with the Tao; to be one with the Tao is to abide forever.*
>
> *Such a one will be safe and whole even after the dissolution of his body.*
>
> Lao Tzu

Along the way everyone benefits fully and happily because God perfectly crafts the universe with the *necessary* laws, rules, procedures, and consequences. If any part of this picture was gone, we wouldn't benefit as much and have confusion instead of harmony.

To understand this need for order and purpose we'll look at a city. Everyone agrees that city laws and rules are meant for everyone's benefit. A person may experience inconvenience at a stop light while late for work, but this consequence is necessary for a safe and efficient flow of traffic. And noisy neighbors face the consequence of fines so others may sleep, even though the few party-goers won't enjoy themselves. Overall though, everyone makes sacrifices and experiences consequences so life will be better than with no laws at all. The most important principle, the goal, is the benefit of the entire city. The highest citizenship and satisfaction becomes the service and sacrifice for others that eventually removes many laws and all overbearing government: Selfless serving gets better results.

Frequently, God requires that we make sacrifices and experience consequences to benefit others. God could ask you to spend your raise in a new way or lead you to tolerate a troublesome neighbor or roommate. It may be that you hurt your body and see a need to change. Or God may direct you to stop ignoring your children and turn the T.V. off. Our loving Father has numerous ways to rouse us and draw us forward. It may be painful or "not fun" but it's necessary and leads to the satisfaction of giving, and ultimately, spiritual growth.

If we willingly break the rules, consequences impact us. Most of us experience these consequences in the form of dissatisfaction, depression, and unhappiness. These feelings and experiences operate for our *benefit* as well as that of others. In reality, these experiences, inside and outside, can become the tools to get us on track again for renewed vigor and happiness by sparking our hearts.

Following God's leadings brings us and others the best life possible, the life of real freedom, spirituality, and happiness. For real emancipation is happiness, not just the ability to do as you please.

These people clarify doing God's will:

> I think the law of the universe is that whatever's useful to the universe in an impersonal way, it cooperates with and helps, finds valuable, makes use of. Obviously God is going to know what those things are; He can see around corners and down the street, and you *can't*.

> The vision that we have in our minds of God is wanting something for us that is less than what we can conceive. What else is it that keeps us from doing God's will? We think we have a better idea . . . This person is so much better. One, loves me more than I love myself, as any parent does, but two, has a much better understanding of my potentials, my problems, everything about me . . . what God wants for me takes in the deepest understanding of myself as well as the broadest understanding of the world.

> And so to do that, to do God's will is to embark on the ultimate adventure and the most exciting life that I could possibly have is the one in which I'm doing God's will. In a life of doing God's will there's no wasted moments . . . I will experience the maximum of what life has to offer when I'm doing God's will. Otherwise, I'm always picking something less; it looks great from here but I can't see very much; I'm only three years old.

> God's will is reality. And if you're not doing reality then you are swimming up stream . . . Going along and finding God in things, finding that blueprint, finding those guideposts along the way, and choosing to incorporate those things when you are in a situation, instead of just doing what's best for me or easiest for me, saying "What's the truth here?" "How can I respond from love

here?" You infuse divinity into your own personality and you grow as an individual and you get satisfaction from situations that normally are just something else that you're plodding through.

There was a tightrope walker a long time ago that was going across Niagara Falls with a guy on his back. And some people cut his stabilizing rope that were angry at him. The tightrope started swaying *wildly*. He told the man on his back "Whatever I do, lean with me; don't fight me; don't try to balance; let me do it." And because the guy did that, even though he felt at times they were gonna fall, they got across.

And that's kind of what God is like, I think. You really close your eyes and trust and it will . . . it happens . . . It's the greatest feeling in the world.

At the same time God lays it out let's also remember that our divine parent is righteous. God follows the laws, rules, and procedures he enforces and doesn't change things just because it would be more enjoyable for Him. The universe rhythms are perfect and eternal, and God is totally consistent in following these rules, using regular methods and allowing consequences to occur.

Whether it be the birth of a star, the brilliance of a rainbow, or a depressing moment, it's because of divine laws. Be completely comforted that God *won't change* these and upholds the integrity of life and unified universe stability. You can count on it!

God won't ask us to do more than we can. He knows what we can handle and how consequences will affect us. When we blunder or intentionally buck universe rules, God is listening and is aware of our sincerity level. He isn't a sadistic totalitarian monarch relishing opportunities to punish His subjects, but instead, a real friend and buddy. God gives mercy if we're sincere and that mercy is best for us.

Most parents know there's a time for consequences and a time for mercy. Often, not giving consequences is an opportunity to help a person progress in a way not possible otherwise. But really, none of us can understand the merciful acts of our divine parent. We only know everything will be fine if we're sincere and take action, and are willing to "face the music," to "reap what we sow."

God and Truth, Beauty, and Goodness

Descriptions can be very revealing. The most flattering words we use to characterize something or someone are descriptions of qualities of truth, beauty, and goodness. These three aspects are *the* essential elements of all we value and the people we admire. Our beautiful, true, and good ideals inhabit our hearts and waft a delicious scent through busy, eventful days. Truth, beauty, and goodness are the standards by which all in science, philosophy, and religion can be judged and compared. Embracing and securing these life threads brings happiness and lasting satisfaction and sustains our efforts to imitate the Almighty.

God is the source of the true, the beautiful, and the good, and all potential thereof. When we experience something as true, beautiful, or good, we're seeing reflections of God. As the source and embodiment of truth, beauty, and goodness, the Creator yearns for us to perceive and imbibe these ideals to progress in living the everyday routine and enjoying the best times. This is the art of living.

As we begin to reflect God, we taste these realities and know more about Him. God is the personification of truth, beauty, and goodness in eternal, infinite perfection. Experiences that contain truth, beauty, and goodness make life worth living, a spiritual life of unending God discovery. Thus, imitating God means becoming a consummate universe artist using the medium and material of your thoughts, feelings, and actions to become a living partial reflection of God, just as the beauty of nature is such a reflection of God.

The religious challenge of this age is to those farseeing and forward-looking men and women of spiritual insight who will dare to construct a new and appealing philosophy of living out of the enlarged and exquisitely integrated modern concepts of cosmic truth, universe beauty, and divine goodness. Such a new and righteous vision of morality will attract all that is good in the mind of man and challenge that which is best in the human soul. Truth, beauty, and goodness are divine realities, and as man ascends the scale of spiritual living, these supreme qualities of the Eternal become increasingly co-ordinated and unified in God, who is love.

The Urantia Book

Since God is the source of truth, beauty, and goodness, it's clear they work together in unity: *God is one.* If we say something is ideally true, it's plain that it's also beautiful and good; things beautiful are true and good; and everything good is also true and beautiful. All things work together for a harmonious life, being interrelated and combined to form an exalted symphony. Since truth, beauty, and goodness come from God, they are, in the end, one thing—a reflection of the perfection and majesty of the divine parent.

Of what value is this discussion of theology, the nature of God? How can we put it to use throughout our lives? Why have we spent time considering it? If we fail to answer these questions, we fail to grow fully; we fail to know God. It's necessary to try to understand God to live happily at peace because *your definition of God is your definition of life and how to live it.* The closer our understanding of God's reality the closer we are to imitating Him and finding happiness by drinking of His supremacy through real living.

Just listen to these thoughts on knowing God:

I think if you know God, you don't need to know anything else. I think if you learn that lesson, there's nothing else you need to know. Once you have God, you have everything. And that's a truth that probably is said so often that it becomes a cliché. It's so totally true.

And I think as people get older over the years I've seen them where they reach the point where they mellow out and talk about being in the presence of God. I think that that's quite true.   Without question, with God you don't need anything else. The more you know about God, the easier it is for you. There's probably no other thing you need to know.

I think studying God is probably the most important thing you can do. The reason is, by studying about God . . . you get to know who God is . . . Sure you get to know God through your personal relationship with God, but that personal relationship is so enhanced when someone else or something else describes to you *their* understanding of God.

Mine is only mine. And everybody else has theirs. So there are billions, trillions, of other understandings of who God is. I think that only when I know everybody's, will I have some sort of real understanding of who God is. To me it's extremely important to study what others, whomever they are, say who God is because otherwise you're just stuck with your own interpretation and your own narrow, or your own personal experience, which is great unto you. It has no breadth to it. It doesn't have the breadth and depth you need in order to really understand God in everybody else's eyes too. And to me that's the key.

After this discussion, I believe we long to understand God for four reasons: We want to imitate Him; we enjoy learning about Him; we want to express our full appreciation; and we need assurance and power for our lives. Everyone has these needs and will find them unmet if they don't meet their Creator.

We strive to understand our beginnings to utilize the past, understand the present, and envision the future. God is our beginning and destiny and it's only though learning more about God that we have the promise of growth.

As we said in Chapter 2, everyone must envision an ideal person, an ultimate end, a goal of existence. This flawless person inevitably is our model because He behaves and thinks in perfect ways we'd like to learn. When we discover and accept the divine picture, we begin the journey of development and adventure but without it lose direction and excitement for life. People who make real progress find this ultimate, ideal person, and can't go wrong copying Him.

Our ideal person, our perfect hero, our faultless model, is God. We're poised to begin an eternal destiny if we seriously attempt the imitation of God. Let's become like Him. The more we understand God, the more we can imitate Him. The more we contact God, the more we'll learn about Him. The more we become like God, the more we'll teach others about Him. And the more others know about God, the more they'll teach us about Him. This process never ends and neither will our lives.

Spiritual Truths

Our Universal Father is
perfect and changeless.

God is absolutely helpful.

God is eternal.

God cares about everyone and everything.

God is true, beautiful, and good.

God follows His rules and is fair.

Seeing God Live

In God's Universe
Chapter 4

O

When you study a gifted athlete or craftsman at work, a real professional, you discover his motivation, abilities, and character, and moreover, out of admiration, you long for his *kind* of fulfillment and success—maturity. Looking at the vastness of God's stupendous creation, we see His fullness and begin to sense His assuring totality and appreciate the artistry and perfect competence of His plan.

Our intense hunger for self-improvement leads to unparalleled adventures and is *only* satiated if we do our best in approaching the imitation of God's perfection. This perfection quest begins in understanding God's perfection.

Our Father's Domain—The Universe
To fathom God more fully, we'll examine His domain—the universe. We must understand that God lives in relation to everything and everyone and isn't a sterile concept in theology or a mechanical constant in physics, but our close and intricately involved helper filled with good humor and parental wisdom.

God is concerned with *every* place; look at a distant galaxy, God has a purpose there; touch the petal of a wet flower, it's part of the plan; comb a child's hair, yet another part of the mosaic of God's universe. On into the endless discoveries of science, art, philosophy, and religion, we'll encounter nothing the Creator doesn't play a role with, nothing that isn't defined by God. But, when looking at these things, we ask how God can be so pervasive and dominant; why is God intensely concerned?

Firstly, all comes from God. The Creator is the source of things within and outside our knowledge and the continuing source of our home—the universe. In every way God is Creator of the universe organism, including stars, gas clouds, other objects, our minds and souls, our dearest friends, and any raw material. Nothing originated outside of God.

> When the Almighty
> happened to bemuse his wisdom
> with playing shoot-the-works,
> he opened with one hand the hot valve
> of absolute energy
> and with the other
> the cold valve
> of absolute time.

>   R. Buckminster Fuller

It's very important to remember that while God is the source of the basic material of life He shouldn't be held responsible for His creatures' misuses of it, nor does He conjure these events. God gives us a *choice;* we can use these tools as we wish, either benefiting or harming ourselves or others. Freewill is the gift of God and He respects our right to choose and thus lets us take a route to experience the consequences of such decisions—good or bad.

We're the architects of our thoughts, feelings, and actions and are responsible for our reactions to life. When it comes to unhappiness, unpleasantness, and dissatisfaction, we should blame ourselves since God isn't responsible for abuses of His gracious gifts. How many times do we bemoan life's circumstances which are so necessary to transform us and reject experiences that bring us eternal life and happiness? How frequently do we swipe at God for our stupidity and stubbornness instead of trying to do our best with pleasant robust hearts?

By using freewill we may utilize our gifts, experiences, and resources to discover and realize our destinies. Because there's no limit to potential progress and joy, we should view the painful and trying circumstances as welcome lessons and *the* doors to growth, the precursors of a meaningful and royal life.

Let's drop in on this person's struggle:

> I think the greatest afflictions that I've had are the divorces that I've been through, when a loved one leaves, especially with children. When that's happened to me (It's happened to me a couple of times.), I think God has helped me to have faith . . . I could have never gotten through them without God, without continuing to pray, continuing to talk to God, continuing to have a positive attitude that everything was going to work out all right and that God had something better for me around the next corner. I just had to pick myself up and go on with life and realize that there was a divine purpose for my life even here in this lowly state of a human being, that He had some kind of a plan and by golly, there was something He wanted me to do, and it wasn't sit around and mope and feel sorry for myself.
>
> Working through my friends, specifically my friends with similar beliefs in God, and my parents and my family (I have a very God-loving family.), really was able to get me through the adversity and able to keep me smiling, so to speak, comfort me in times of sorrow, especially those times of sorrow which . . . when you lose a loved one who dies, that's one thing. And when you lose loved ones who walk away and when you have family . . . it's very difficult to work through. Point in fact, worked out best in the end.

> Having been through some of those really difficult
> experiences, difficult times in life, and then coming out
> the other side and having it work out best in the end, I
> realize that it *always* can work out best in the end. It
> depends on how you look at it.

So when we survey the world and list its flaws and imperfections, we must remember most are products of humankind. Frequently we hurt others (No one can forget brutality and senseless conflict.) and ignore the spiritual solution at hand, tempted to think that God, a good God, will come in with broom and mop. But God's plan calls for *us* to do it with His internal help, requiring faith and the exercise of bravery and diligence. Our stamina will come from spiritual satisfaction, our success from growth.

In the end, our days done, we'll take only memories of love, courage, and spiritual growth: This is all that matters. Pain and confusion will melt away since the spirit memory was never harmed and selects the good that will help in the afterlife. Tribulation is for our benefit and actually should make us feel *privileged* to have such crowning progress. For truly, the first shall be last, and least will be greatest. This is part of God's purpose for us within the purpose of the universe.

Examining this dependent and reflective universe, we should ponder that it's completely maintained and structured by God. While we mainly see matter and energy as God's gift of life for us, there are surely other reasons God creates it. And to take God out of its center would mean the instantaneous end since everything is supported and maintained by His physical, mental, and spiritual laws.

Everything came from God. Our thoughts and decisions would be impossible unless God gave us minds to live in the world. The endearing friendships and the sense that we know we're alive (that we know that we know) is God's gift of self-consciousness or personality. From the tiniest grain of sand to an astounding supernova, from handshake to eagle's cry, from a sunset to a marriage, everything is constructed of material once unrealized from God. Therefore, everything and everyone owes existence and continued life to God who is infinite.

As a child, did you ever stand in front of the bathroom mirror and hold up another mirror, peering, trying to see the last tiny mirror within a mirror? Each image became smaller and smaller as you looked deeper and deeper into mystery. You craned your neck to peer intensely and more closely into the shrinking mirrors, trying to see infinity . . . And isn't it easy to look into the night sky and think about God's infinity with innumerable stars shining and dancing. Furthermore, if we look at all people, in all times, in all places, in all walks of life, none are identical. Again, another example of God's infinity.

Everything God creates comes from an *unending* supply, whether it be people or stars. This means our lives can always be refreshing and different, with new experiences, discoveries, friends and relationships, and understandings. Besides being infinite, God is eternal; God has always been around and always will be. This is difficult to understand since everything we know about has a strict beginning, middle, and final end, *period.* Just think! Our loving Creator never began; He never created Himself or was created; *in no way can we apply the past tense to God.*

For God, there's no time, only a succession of events. Time and space came from God and are used by Him to help us live. The meaning of an eternal God is that He simply **IS** ("I AM."). Even with our time-bound minds, we realize it couldn't be otherwise since there must be a source for everything that didn't come from something else, one independent of time and space. The timeless, infinite God is simultaneously the most loving being in the universe and the most incomprehensible. He is a complete mystery; we can't use logic, intuition, or experience to explain God. Eternity and infinity aren't part of earthly experience but are necessary to make it possible.

If God weren't infinite and eternal, we wouldn't be here. Our minds are taxed trying to understand the mystery of God. Let's face it, God is beyond our comprehension no matter how advanced we become or how far along in the eternal future we are. We know what kind of person God is and can experience Him daily, but never will we understand everything about Him, especially His eternal-infinite nature.

Do this person's thoughts sound familiar?

> The most incomprehensible thing about God is how God can be aware of *every single thing* that's going on in *every single* person's mind at one time and know what's going on *everywhere* throughout the entire universe, is just totally incomprehensible to me. How He can be aware what's going on in my mind and be *totally* there and loving and understanding and be there with me and be that way for every single person on this planet, the five billion people, and the *trillions* and *zillions* of beings throughout the entire universe, past present and future, of all different mortals, etc., and keep all that together is just totally incomprehensible. I cannot fathom that at all.
>
> I can barely keep up with what I am doing. How He does it, and does it with seemingly no effort, it's just a part of innateness, and then does it with His attitude and His nature, and sees the whole picture from the parts, and also participates in all the parts, throughout eternity, *at once*, is just . . . I can't figure that one out. I probably never will be able to figure that one out. I accept it. I worship it. It's incomprehensible.

But don't feel bad. It's fine to be human and flabbergasted! You and the universe have a purpose, *so does your confusion and awe*. We're certainly part of a stupendous destiny because of the Father's love, the infinite everlasting kindness of the Creator. When we look at this world, we can be assured it's under control and heading toward a better future, no matter how discouraging or baffling things are.

We don't understand everything, most things, but we'll learn more and more as time goes by. We're children of God on the divine stage.

Trust.

God's Attributes

Just as we have the tools of body and mind, God uses tools He created to carry out His plan. With these attributes, God concerns Himself with the universe and makes sure His purpose is being achieved, that His will is done. But despite the fact that He's mobilizing such power and activities, God is here for all of us, in all of us, making sure our needs are met. This is the intriguing recital of God's attributes.

Let's begin with God's ability to be everywhere. Our understanding of life informs us that we can only be in one location at a time and must find transportation and make arrangements to get to it. But God is all places at the same time. In addition, while God is able to be everywhere at the same time—*omnipresent*—His home is at the center of the universe, and as the source point for God, doesn't change. He saturates the universe and its beings with His caressing presence.

Through the many beings in the universe, God stays everywhere at all times. Even deep inside we simple humans, God lives to split the darkness in every distressing moment. On all stars and blades of grass the presence of God dances. Doubtless, God has other techniques to be in all places at all times and doubtless this omnipresence is necessary for God to execute his plan.

> *The usual conception of God as one single being outside of the world and behind the world is not the beginning and the end of religion . . . The true nature of religion is neither this idea nor any other, but immediate consciousness of the Deity as He is found in ourselves and in the world.*

> Friedrich Schleiermacher

God's presence takes *different forms* according to the many places it may be from a human to a mountain, but it's not the same as what it surrounds and permeates. God may be on the island or lie in your mind, but He isn't your mind or part of the island. I believe His presence is all-encompassing and interwoven with things and people and varies accordingly with the needs of the person or the requirements of the object.

And yet, as far-reaching as God's presence and activities are, He stays in one place, the center of the universe, and never forgets himself or is diluted. God simply wants to be with His created beings and places in order to carry out His mandates and love His living children while maintaining the stability and foundation of the universe.

Simultaneous with omnipresence is God's ability to know about everything, everywhere, at the same time; God is *omniscient*. He knows all in the past, present, and future, even down to the "hairs on your head." This knowledge is essential for God to ensure universe progress and the satisfaction of its beings for the present and the future. The Universe Creator knows everything that will ever happen throughout eternal time and the succession of events and ensures His children can live valuable and interesting lives individually and collectively *forever*.

While we accept and are impressed by God's knowledge of the big things, we shouldn't forget that our Creator knows what's going on inside us even before we do. In fact, we're much more aware of this fact than of the innumerable agencies God employs in universe administration. There's nothing that escapes the attention of the Universal Father, but we're most comforted by the fact that He knows and dwells in us.

This means you can count on God to help you and know your feelings, to know what you're going through. Although there's no part of your life the Creator doesn't know about and fully understand, of most significance to Him are your intentions and decisions. He wants to know if you're making spiritual decisions as much as you can, everywhere you can. We should remember that God is only concerned with our spiritual achievements and intentions—our striving—and He strongly desires our celestial growth and happiness. Consequently, He wants us to help those around us to progress and know Him at the same time we pursue our family, individual, and career goals.

Recalling that God is the source of all, let's also realize He has complete power over everything and uses it to carry out His plan. Nothing evades His influence. Despite this power, God respects our *freewill* and lets us make decisions and experience their good and bad repercussions. God is not one to step in and stop us when we've made a decision, albeit He continually tries to show us the better way.

Let's listen to these thoughts:

> God is the granter of freewill, the great granter of freewill. One of the whole points of experiencing life is to make decisions, on your own. I talk to God about my decisions at great length. I don't talk to Him as much about my material decisions as I do about spiritual decisions or quasi spiritual decisions. I ask for strength in being able to make material decisions that will help me out.

Throughout this vast universe and our lives, it's tempting to think God is aloof and uninvolved, no longer in charge. However, like any good parent, God is infinitely concerned with our spiritual welfare and is constantly directing His creation to *become* better, not merely to be better. In orchestrating this immense panorama of change, God uses the technique of evolution on physical, mental, and spiritual levels.

People, life, and matter change gradually or suddenly based on progress in stress. All life faces the challenge of surviving. If we respond and work with God, we evolve into better people and thus ensure our spiritual survival although we're certain our bodies are meant only for life here on earth. Our divine parent beckons us to real spiritual places with adventure and our desires: This is God's style.

I think it's easy to be overly concerned (After all, we're talking about life and death here.), but don't be; all that needs to be done is being done to help us grow spiritually in the midst of change in an evolving eternal universe of stability and purpose. The raw materials of life will be there for us to create delight, progress, satisfaction, and eternal life.

God's Will

As we move forward to understand God the person we must remember that one of the most important characteristics of an individual is *will*, the ability to make decisions and act. This involves the way we think, what we think about, and how long we think about it. A decision is the full use of will that results in action; we do something. Most of these decisions of thinking and using our bodies are for a *reason,* a goal, whether we realize it or not. People do things for reasons and so does God.

Since God is the perfect unlimited person, His will is perfect and unlimited. You know, most of us change our goals and desires on a constant basis as well as our approach to them. Also, we vary the time we spend on them. But please remember, God does not! The Father's goal and purpose is the same and won't change because He knows precisely the reason for His creation and uses exact methods to achieve it *for all time*. God knows the result and has a plan to make it occur.

I believe our divine Parent's will is unlimited and operates in two ways according to the situation: First, God has a perfect divine way of doing things and wants this *way* used—VALUE. For example, if I went over to help a friend work on his car, there's a definite way God would like me to behave to help my friend. He may want me to be tolerant, courteous, tactful, patient, and honest, but isn't concerned whether we use Penzoil® or Castrol Oil®, but rather the way we get along and approach doing the job. He's concerned with values that help us achieve the greatest good to meet the most needs for the most people for the longest time.

Following the way is the *what* of God's will, the specifics. At times (only we know which) God has something He would like us to do, something to be done *specifically*. This is the precise part of God's will where His plan is helped most by the *what* in addition to the way. God may want you specifically to leave your career and start new work or he may ask you to go next door and see how a neighbor is faring. It's important to remember that there are no limits on what God might want done.

Here's what these people think:

> I like to think God's will dominates my life. I try to make that happen. If that's true, then I've succeeded. There's not a day goes by that I'm not concerned about God's will, doing the right thing. But it's incumbent on anything that I attempt. Some of the challenges, big decisions I've had recently . . . I'd be very dismayed at myself if I'd chosen wrong. And I've asked for Him to set me straight if I do pick wrong. It's everything to me . . . that's what you're trying to do.

> God's will only operates to the extent that you allow it. It can be an unconscious choice. You don't recognize the Father's will working in your life until retrospectively,

from a spiritual point of view, you look for it. I suspect that there are people who live their entire lives here and don't do that. People who recognize that they're sons of God should do that and they should do it regularly to recognize the growth that they achieved from doing the Father's will.

That's just a way of keeping track of who you are. The more you become like God, the more you need to recognize it, not just for your own benefit, but to recognize that you're on course. The Spirit that lives within us . . . there's a wonderful example of this indwelling Spirit. Sometimes it's so subtle that you're attempting to do the Father's will and you don't really recognize it. It's like you're asleep on a vessel at sea and during the night the captain changes course. At some point in the future you recognize that "I'm on this new heading, and it's great." It takes time and a sense of awareness of what's happening in your life.

Later in the book we'll learn how to find God's will, but these examples are *attempts* to understand His will; these aren't the absolute truth about God. All in all though, we know God's will is perfect and will lead to the best possible world for ourselves, our families, and everyone else.

The Will of God

I worship thee, sweet will of God!
And all thy ways adore;
And every day I live, I long
To love thee more and more.

When obstacles and trials seem
Like prison-walls to be,
I do the little I can do,
And leave the rest to thee.

He always wins who sides with God
To him no chance is lost:
God's will is sweetest to him when
It triumphs at his cost.

Ill that God blesses is our good,
And unblest good is ill;
And all is right that seems most wrong,
If it be His dear will!

Frederick William Faber

God's will adjoins every part of our lives and every function of the universe. There is a perfect and divine way to do everything and there are specific things that should be done; *God's will is the best way to do things and the best things to do* and will achieve His purpose and provide us with the best life, outstripping our dreams. We may think we know best, but there's always a better way and a better thing to do—God's will.

God's Attitude

Feeling, thinking, and reacting in certain ways to certain things is a constant part of life. An attitude is a feeling toward someone or something and also what we would like to happen in that instance; it's an *intention* toward someone, something, or ourselves. Our attitudes result in actions, decisions we carry out, things we do. It's helpful to think of God in the same way, having attitudes, for He has intentions toward us and everything.

The most important aspect of God is **LOVE,** the first and most significant thing to remember: **He loves you perfectly under any circumstances!** This supreme God attitude pervades all His actions. Everything we think limits this attitude should be ejected in the journey inward with God. It's time to base our ideas about God's love on our inner experience with Him and promptly scrap any idea which obscures His love.

We have so many misuses of the word love that it's important to understand the meaning of God's love. God's love is His intention to do good to us, His willingness to give of Himself completely for our happiness and spiritual growth. Love is, then, a willingness and a desire to help other *people* while forgetting yourself. If you don't have these two things, it's not love, not unselfish service, not God's love.

We feel wonderful loving others, but love is *action and intention* not mere feeling. God is love and is dominated by this desire to help His children while giving of Himself to any degree necessary. This is His willingness to do everything needed even though we may not understand or like it at the time (like a crying child). We would do well to cleanse our idea of love by adopting God's attitude toward us.

Many times we don't help a friend for one reason or another. We may be experiencing too much pain or have other justifications for withholding God's love. It seems we come up with a full array of defenses to protect us from change, from becoming like God. Loving like God is an act of the highest *courage* and requires an ongoing dedication to surmount laziness and inertia as well as fear of rejection.

Throughout our lives we treat ourselves according to standards and judge ourselves by those goals. Sometimes we feel that if we haven't performed, we don't deserve help. And frequently we apply the same attitude to others because they haven't performed. The attitude of our day states that a person gets things by working hard and doing well and should be supported only if they succeed. But there's something distasteful and foul here. Let's not make this mistake and let's not assume God operates this way.

Our Father gives His love continuously to everyone in beneficial ways. The Universal Father's love never follows the attitudes of a selfish world or a prejudiced mind but extends even while we withhold it, ignore God, hurt others, or slow things down. God's love is fragrant, constant, eternal, and abundant. There are no requirements to receive it.

Let's listen in on these thoughts:

It's unbelievable to know that God loves me no matter what I do, in any circumstance. It's astounding, it's just wonderful to know that He loves me so much without requiring *anything* in return. It doesn't matter what kind of week I have: I can go out and be very spiritual, paying attention to His will, helping other people, and I experience a profound love. The next week I can go out and just forget that He's there, and forget about being on the path and living with His love. His love is *still there* in the same way! it's still there! I experience it when I listen and am ready for it. It's just *there*. It's not like any human relationship I've ever experienced.

With friends, or people you meet, it just seems that they have some kind of hidden agenda and they're looking for something: "You scratch my back, I'll scratch yours." So many human relationships go awry that way because someone is expecting something, and when they don't get it, they get angry. They just withhold their love because the admission price hasn't been paid.

God's love is not like that. God's love is total and encompassing. It shoots right through you and vivifies your life. I treasure God's love more than anything. I want to learn to love like *He* loves.

I knew that God loved me and that I loved Him. But, I always felt it was a non-personal thing; I was about as important as a grain of sand on the beach. I was there, but I wasn't important; I had no part; I was just here. There were great leaders and great spiritual people and people that had accomplished a lot that were important to Him but I was *nothing*.

When I found out that I was indeed important to God, it made me feel complete."

Think of it, God is in you **now** waiting to touch you if you would listen. Suppose you think of part of your life you feel bad about, or dissatisfied with, or envision a time when you hurt another. Right now and always there's a vast unending reservoir of love waiting to enter your pained and confused mind and quench its yearning. God is ready.

> *The Father's love follows us now and throughout the endless circle of the eternal ages. As you ponder the loving nature of God, there is only one reasonable and natural personality reaction thereto: You will increasingly love your Maker; you will yield to God an affection analogous to that given by a child to an earthly parent; for, as a father, a real father, a true father, loves his children, so the Universal Father loves and forever seeks the welfare of his created sons and daughters.*
>
> *The Urantia Book*

God's love is not just for soothing, but a revelation of yourself and what needs to be done to progress and be happy. God loves you and is stern when needed. Frequently we creep down to slack living and selfish tendencies that require this divine remedy, this cold plunge. But don't get the misconception that God gets angry. No matter how many times you make the same mistake, or even intentionally hurt others, God's love is constant and always there for you.

Not only does God love you with no strings attached, but He forgives your mistakes even before you realize it or ask. Our Creator's understanding is so absolute that He cannot but love us since our true intentions and ambitions are plain, not just our less-than-successful attempts to be like Him.

We're released from the claws of fear and inaction and brought to a new level of understanding, blasting every obstruction to a relationship with God, finding a life of fulfilling adventure and endless accomplishment. There's no good reason to think God doesn't allow for our mistakes or misunderstands the nature of human progress. Our Creator is all-forgiving and completely willing to give us another chance as we travel through life's experiences.

God's love is the love of a Father for His family—those dependent on Him for support and guidance. And while God is so great and majestic, may we not forget He's tender and always trying to reach into our lives. All of us can honestly **feel** the Creator's love just like we experience anything else in life. If you sincerely crave this touch and spend time with God and serve others, you'll feel Him. The love of God is the greatest experience of life and will continue to be so into eternity no matter what we may be doing.

Deep within us, though, comes the gloom of fear and misunderstanding of God, affecting every action and attempt to know Him. Early on, our forbearers envisioned God as a personification of nature's elements, and later, part of the ghost-spirit world. The gods mankind created were cruel and unyielding, just like his early environmental experiences and the cultures in which he found himself enmeshed.

As time went on, gradual changes in our God-concept occurred just as society changed and improved. Finally, the highest concept of God was brought by Jesus, revealed in his *life* which opened the world's eyes to the true nature of God, a loving divine parent who relates to each person. Men and women aren't pawns of terrestrial forces or celestial vagaries, but cherished sons and daughters of a loving Father.

Our highest concept of God begins with our highest concept of a human being and must be based on human relationships in the ideal sense. God is an absolutely loving, perfect, divine parent, always willing to give us all we need in unending patience and gentle affection. The attitude of the Father is one of a perfect parent who understands His children entirely and wishes them to do their best. He delights in seeing them grow through life, through joys and agonies, and finally, the glories. *God is better than your most ideal concept of Him.*

And this is where we started in this chapter. Any human negative aspects we attach to God will evaporate as we discover a living inner experience of the Creator. We must be willing to seek the truth in whatever form it comes and from whatever source. The Creator is always attempting to show us the truth about Himself and the way we should live. The *greatest satisfaction* is to be with God and know His love while working nobly, intensely, wholeheartedly, and steadfastly. This is the core of The Universal Religion.

Can we know what this means? can we throw off the prejudices and uncomfortable experiences of the past? will we act with rigidity and skepticism or with open intelligence and faith to God for a divine embrace?

God gives us so much, has done so much, let's embrace Him in an everlasting partnership and understand who He really is, ever allowing for our ideas about Him to change as we change. We're the daughters and sons of the loving Creator who put us here for a reason; let's not forget, but instead seek God every day to learn more about Him, together. Let's release our minds from the encumbrances of bad experiences and stubbornness to see God now.

Think about the wonder and majesty of God, His truth, beauty, and goodness. We feel good and secure when we're working for a good firm, live in a beautiful area, come from a prestigious school or institution, have good investors, and when our friends and family get behind us . . .

. . . Feel the joy; swim in the delight of life with God! You have as *your* Father the most influential, powerful, helpful, loving, understanding being in the universe, the absolute designer, planner, and Creator. He is on your side and will do everything for your spiritual benefit and wants you to succeed and be happy. He feels for you when you encounter burdens and pains and revels in your accomplishments with you. **God is on your side!**

This person has an interesting perspective:

> If you're on God's side, you find out there is no side. You're not fighting evil; you're only creating good. You're not contending with anybody, you're only trying to give an alternative. As soon as you get into that, you find out there's nothing to fight, only things to create.
>
> If I'm on His side, there is no other side. That's freedom from contending with anything . . . that's great freedom, that's great creativity. And that's a wonderful state to be in. It takes a long time for me to learn anything. It's fairly recent that I've gotten that through my head. Don't fight anything. Just give an alternative that people are able to pick. If people are able to pick that, fine. If they don't, that's fine.

What a wonder! What intense freeing knowledge! Let's go out with it and realize everything will work out for the best if we're sincere. This is God's will. We're the children of a perfect God and should find assurance and peace in this fact; *in all* agonies and through every disappointment, with every joy and satisfaction, God is with us and will show us the way in spiritual security.

Think of God's resources, power, and wisdom; think of His unlimited strength and caring for us; think of His infinite knowledge; think of His perfection. Wow! Nothing can hurt us spiritually; nothing can change our destiny; if we sincerely desire to know and be like God, sincerely desire to serve and love others, then life is our oyster and God will help us open it.

No fear or problem can improve without God; all life's experiences can be utilized for growth since we have spiritual favor with God. Yes, life is hard, often brutally cruel, frustrating, and confusing, maybe even unfair, but given the knowledge God has, given the opportunities for growth and achievement, would we want otherwise? Aren't we privileged? It's time to celebrate this knowledge of God and His love for us, the life beyond our imagination. It's time to invigorate and scintillate not only on the mountains of achievement but also the plains of patient cultivation.

It's time to enroll in the divine school to remake ourselves and our world.

Spiritual Truths

Our heavenly Father creates
and controls the universe perfectly.

God is infinite and unlimited.

God is omnipresent, omniscient,
and omnipotent.

God's will is the perfect plan for the
universe and each person.

God loves unconditionally.

Relating to God

You Can Touch God
Chapter 5

○

After our extended and challenging discussion of God, it's time for the experience of experiences; it's time we examine how to relate to God and then fulfill the edifying potential of these techniques. But, how can I emphasize the significance of knowing God one-to-one? Is it possible to verbalize this matchless beauty and perfect joy? I doubt it, but I'll try to fuel your explorations.

A relationship with God is *everything* and will remain so —an end in itself and the reason for your existence. Your union with God, while being a source of unlimited divine vision and thought, is interconnected with other relationships and somewhat determined by them. Let us explore this experience and strive to live for it with riveting expectancy of the unrevealed spiritual delights of our unseen Father.

God is Knowable
With finality, let's realize the Creator is knowable. **God is the most real experience!** It's impossible to prove God is inside you or that He created the universe, but you'll know when you know and be able to withstand all contrary

persuasions, inspite their sophistication. After this experience, your life will be remade, transported to God's reality.

Not only is God knowable, but He's a person to converse with, love, feel with, and learn about, the gentlest, most understanding, most loving person. Think of it! All the rewards of any relationship can be yours with God. This is true! This is possible! If you want to know God, you can and will (And in fact, you *already* experience Him.).

As a matter of fact, God is seeking you and wants you to experience Him. He desires you to increasingly feel His presence and live His love and is longing to make contact with you in all moments, no matter what your circumstances or state of mind; God loves regardless of economic, political, religious, social, or other status because He gives *equal* standing to His sincere children. The Father will do all to help you perceive Him for He has the greatest caring and concern, an unconditional love. He patiently waits with transcending touch.

Remember your most treasured experiences, the most valuable moments, and comprehend that there's a dimension of joy and satisfaction much greater than these. **God is the greatest experience.** Everything else is a means to this end since touching the infinite parent is the most rewarding, intriguing, and unending adventure. While we may be distracted by many worldly complexities, this watershed of majesty awaits us, quivering to be released.

Let's listen to these people:

> To experience God is to feel a wholeness and purity that I haven't experienced before in my life. It's to know that there is a superior consciousness and love that's present, that's all loving and all trusting.
>
> In my everyday life I work in a busy office: I have a busy job. And there are times when I can stop and look through the craziness of a hectic day and feel that

presence and know there's more to life than what we
see, that there is a God who loves us.

For me it is an assurance, a feeling of warmth, a
feeling of being nurtured, a feeling of being cared for,
ministered to, just as carefully and lovingly as anybody
else is, regardless of what their status is. It's a feeling of
peace and assurance that everything's gonna be O.K.

Our goal then, is to find and comprehend God. It's
necessary we learn to do His will each moment, in every
decision, through all thought. In this quest you'll give God a
name that describes your unique comprehension of Him
based on your direct experience of His Spirit. As you strive
through life's simple and complex problems God will give
what you require along with a fuller and fuller revelation of
Himself.

It's funny; we seem to have the ability and propensity to
create unneeded frustrations and complications. Many times
we simply don't see the right way and stubbornly keep going
. . . sometimes over the edge—crisis—waiting until the last
second to try alternatives. Even though the answer is staring
us in the face, and we *know* it's right, we persist in outmoded
patterns of living and thought.

We do this most with God. Although the truth of God is
in us and attainable, we insist on running full-speed ˙to
oblivion, depression, loneliness, and confusion. Human
beings have made the God-quest a seemingly difficult and
dehydrated pursuit, an unusual activity reserved for spiritual
experts and dreamy mystics. While we've apparently made
the God-quest confusing, complex, unreasonable, and distant,
it isn't like this.

God makes the search for Him simple and supplies
everything necessary because He cares for us and understands
us like any kind parent. As we'll see, the steps to knowing
our Father are quite simple (understandable by the youngest)

and refreshing—sensible spiritual habits for all. Truly, the more we understand the Father's majestic and liberating ascension plan, the more we thank Him for being in charge and the more astounded we are at the unimagined rewards of doing His will.

While you won't find God looking here or there, you will find Him by looking *inside,* because at your core lives a piece of God that's with you continually. When you seek and find God within, you've experienced God's touch and made the greatest discovery. Discovering and continually experiencing God within is *religion*—your religion. He was always there; He is here before and after we begin searching for Him.

It's simple, straightforward, and completely feasible because God designed it that way. It may seem that we have to do elaborate tricks to find God, but really, He's kind and provides a clear crisp path, not a tangled and mired maze; our God is not in hiding. **You always have Him in and with you.**

Now, it's easy to understand that a loving God could be so logical and provide a fair program, but why does it seem so hard to know Him and grow? As obvious as a sunrise, trying to communicate with God is quite strenuous. While it's apparent our journey to God is clear, it's also obvious that it's hard and demanding. This isn't a soft bed of hopeful longing but a noble quest for self-mastery requiring hard work and difficult decisions.

If you look at a newborn and its parents as an analogy to our relationship with God, the tension is immediately clear. We're simply not able to have direct conversations (that is, both ways) with God because of *who we are.* Our present inability to hear God's direct voice is due to our stage of development, our immaturity and finiteness, our limitations. Right now we have limited capacities to experience God's leadings and must patiently await direct contact.

Simply, when you compare the thoughts of God to ours, it's easy to see why we can't understand or know them directly. However, this isn't the real impediment because most of us either ignore our leadings or avoid spiritual decisions that open our minds to such God-experiences. The main interference is our periodic selfishness and laziness, living that closes our minds and eventually dulls our hearts to the voice and touch of our Father. We aren't victims of a cosmic setup with blinders on our eyes or cotton in our ears, but instead, evolving children with expected immature tendencies.

These people speak of a common experience:

> I've impeded communication by just being very self-centered. It's real easy. I went through a period of years and years and years . . . I became very self-centered and decided that I had to go out and look out for myself and achieve things, and all that type of thing.
>
> Once you become self-centered and ego-driven, it just impedes your relationship with God . . . if you're self-centered as opposed to other-centered. At least that's how I experience it. So I have been slowly pulling myself out of that for about the last ten years just to get myself back to being other-centered. Trying to be as conscious as I can of my fellow man.
>
> It's a slow process. And the reason it's such a slow process is that I was ego-centered for so long. That doesn't mean I stopped believing in God, but I didn't *act* as though I believed in God. There's a difference.

> We continuously impede communication with God. I think that basically we impede communication with God by being fearful. I impede communication with God, firstly, by not allowing myself to hear God, constantly cluttering my life with sound. Most people cannot deal with silence. And one can't experience the fullness of communication with God without silence.

In this day and age it's mass communication: So we've got the T.V.s going; we've got the radios, the music's going . . . that would be major.

We spend so much time being fearful that we shut out any communication that we might somehow reach with God because we're so damned fearful and we live too much in terror. Again, I say "we" because I don't think I'm unique in that. I think this is one of the reasons that people are so fearful of silence. It's *fear*.

And then there's drugs, and alcohol, and there's filling one's mind with the usual tripe and trivia our days are full of. These are all factors that impede communication with God . . . Television's runnin' all the time; you're on the phone all the time—it's our inability to be silent. I say we—*me*. This is the reason that mass media's so popular. These are the things that keep us from communicating with God.

We get into bad habits. Faith and spiritual growth is something that's developed: You're not just born with it and then you forget about it. It's something you feel drawn to and then you either develop that or you don't. The more you develop it, the more communication you are having with God. If you don't develop it, you fill it with the other (nonsense), the noise, the this, all the distractions that we all fill our lives with, that I fill my life with.

The difficulty in spiritual growth is that I have to break my habits, I have to reorient my habits to put myself in a frame of mind and circumstances whereby I can communicate with God.

There is, deep within our minds, a piece of God that's our phone line, our personal contact with the Creator. Each of us has a unique part of God that guides and strengthens us daily, that provides constant contact and communication with God. This Spirit of God is the source of our experience of God and the *only* real proof of His existence.

This Spirit guide from God is a personal friend, a divine cheerleader, a loving mate, and our assurance of eternal life as children of God. As a renewer and energizer, your individual Spirit friend is unmatched and is dedicated to helping you know God and do His will; this indwelling spirit is the channel of God's love and guidance and, as you can know God, you can know this personal guide. This brings us to the essentials of knowing God.

Most people would like to experience God more (This is obvious.). The key is extremely easy to understand, yet requires going past logic and acting on a *recognition of truth* because you must trust your experience of God and learn to recognize all future experiences. The fact is, you know when you know something is true and real. So when you have this feeling about God, act on it and observe what happens; trust the most real of experiences.

Simply take the **time** *to pour your heart out to the Father, listen, and then ask for courage and strength to act on this guidance.* Do this each day and you'll know God and grow. Nothing else will suffice.

Experiencing God is not a fantasy of the mind, but the most mind-transcending experience possible. Our minds are the tools of our hearts. Listen to your heart. It knows the truth and tells your mind when something is true. This Creator-contact is the most intimate, personal, and sublime reality that can come into our lives.

> *Men all too often forget that God is the greatest experience in human existence. Other experiences are limited in their nature and content, but the experience of God has no limits save those of the creature's comprehension capacity, and this very experience is in itself capacity enlarging. When men search for God, they are searching for everything. When they find God, they have found everything. The search for God is the unstinted bestowal of love attended by amazing discoveries of new and greater love to be bestowed.*
>
> *The Urantia Book*

You know, it's sad that this glorious experience has frequently been relegated to hushed conversations or withheld expressions. Instead, it should be the focus of all we do, the reason for being alive, the reward for seeking the truth—God's presence. How many times are we encouraged (*enthusiastically with vigor*) to know God's presence each day? Why is so little emphasis placed on this, the greatest experience of life? It's time for us to learn to quiet our minds and lives to feel God's touch today and tomorrow, for all todays and tomorrows.

Feeling the presence of God (learning to recognize and savor it) is the most important part of contacting God. It's possible to feel God's love daily and for longer, more extended periods throughout the day. In fact, as time goes on, this will become the delightful, comforting, edifying norm for you. This is the perfect experience!

Your Relationship with God

Do we ever grasp the fact that we can have a one-to-one friendship/relationship with the Father? Just as you can know your best friend alone and privately, enjoying secrets and shared experiences, you can know God.

We first and most importantly know God as individuals, person to person. As the children of God, we can always talk to this divine parent and know our true needs have already been provided for and will continue to be supplied. What are friends for?

If you know God as a friend, it's because you've found Him within yourself. The importance of this friendship is deeply significant. Just as the stem of a flower provides the basic elements for growth, and as a dam creates the stability and size of a reservoir, friendship with our Father accelerates our mighty spiritual growth stimulus and sustains us. Such a relationship with such a person is the most sublime and satisfying relationship, the purpose of our lives. Nothing should take precedence.

Here are some thoughts about a relationship with God:

My relationship with God affects my life so profoundly, it colors the way I interact with people; it colors my conscious choice. Most of the time I definitely err and forget, but I try every moment I can to think about what the Father would have me do or what would be a God-like, Christ-like thing to do.

Recently in my office, I was in a meeting and there was a case where a person that I work with took credit for something that I had done. Instead of feeling anger toward her and being upset, I realized she was coming from a place where she was feeling insecure and needed to say that to make herself feel better. And I just had this flow of love that was God inspired saying; "This is not important; it's really O.K.; just love her. You're getting your job done."

It makes a difference when we start feeling that kind of love and wisdom. We allow it to come through. And the more I do it, the more I can do it. Like learning to ride a bicycle or learning a sport. In a way, it's learning to seek God's wisdom and guidance . . . "Not my will but your will be done."

I'm in telemarketing (In other words, I'm spending a lot of time on the phone.) selling product that most people are not interested in. Thusly there's a tremendous amount of rejection in it. One can become very sensitized. When I start the day out with a good meditation and I spend some good good time, *quality* time with God in the morning, the day starts out usually very, very successful because all my guards are down. I'm very open; I'm enjoying what I'm doing; and I'm actually communicating rather than trying to B.S. The more in tune I am, the more successful I become in my business. And that plays out in every aspect of life . . .

. . . the more in tune you are, the better everything is; the more spiritual, the closer you are to God, the better off you are in every aspect of life. You even rest better.

Since God knows best and is fully devoted to us, it's only sensible that our loyalty and obedience should go to Him. **Trying to know God and do His will must be the ultimate priority.** All human authorities and experiences outside our God experience should be measured, tested, and superseded by God's instructions and illumination.

When we know God's in us we know things work out right in our spiritual development. Your trust in God can be absolute; you can be sure of God. Of course, God doesn't guarantee you'll receive the treasures or wishes you crave, but promises happiness and spiritual growth if you cooperate. The ideal future is not imaginable but *unimaginable*, hence requiring faith to grasp its reality and our cooperation with the unseen. This collaboration is possible only when we trust the Father and let go of the sure, predictable paths which never lead to the faith-future, the unseen destiny.

In addition to faith in the unseen, things that work for other relationships work for this one; the same benefits can be had, and more, perfectly. If you've had a nice walk with a friend, you should try it with God; if sharing a quiet sunset was nice with your spouse, try it with God; if you cried to a friend about a failure, try it with God; when you burst with the thrill of success and just have to tell a friend, try it with God. When in doubt try it with God!

Have you ever realized the wonder of the friendship you can have with Me? Have you ever thought what it means to be able to summon at will the God of the World?

Even with a privileged visitor to an earthly king there is the palace ante-chamber, and the time must be at the pleasure of the king.

But to My subjects I have given the right to enter My Presence when you will, nay more they can summon Me to bedside, to workshop — and I am there.

> *Could Divine Love do more? Your nearest earthly friend cannot be with you on the instant. Your Lord, Your Master, your Divine Friend — Yes.*
>
> *When men seek to worship me they think of the worlds I rule over, of creation, of mighty law and order — and then they feel the awe that precedes worship.*
>
> *To you I say feel awe, feel the desire to worship Me in wondering amazement. But think too of the mighty, tender, humble condescension of My Friendship. Think of Me in the little things of everyday life.*
>
> *God Calling*

As we said, you must put in time and effort and act on *faith*; this is your growth-partnership with God. If you're not willing to risk living with God, then God can't become your focus or satisfy your needs. When you really take time and make God a priority, then this relationship may never end. It's up to you.

How to Know God

O. K. Let's take a look at what works to know and touch God daily. What are the habits that open our minds to God and where should our efforts focus? It's time to find out.

Attitude is everything. Your mind and heart are a channel opened and closed by the simple action of your attitude. Your attitude is the way you intend to act toward people and experiences. This attitude will make the difference in whether you experience God or not.

If you sincerely want to find God, you *already* have. But, to get to know God, you must love Him with all your faculties and knowledge. There is no other way! Love God for who He is, not His powers and ability. The way to God is by living love everywhere in life, with yourself, others, and God.

Be a powerful and determined glacier, carving channels of light in your mind with sincerity and determination, allowing God's bounties to flow. Make time for God; take *long* rests to experience Him and then determine to live what you've learned. This done, the ecstasy and momentum of your newly awakened self will fill your mind to the brim and saturate your life.

These people know the value of determination:

> It's important to be persistent because there are a lot of distractions around. There is an incredible number of ways in which the society in which we live would divert you from the path of knowing God and pursuing a relationship with Him, everything from television to advertising, all the other distractions.
>
> And I think you have to be very persistent not to get caught up in all of those other things that go on on a daily basis. It's hard work in some respects. If I get caught up in those things I flop back into my ego orientation and more of a selfish me, what's in it for me? orientation. I stop thinking about other people and start worrying about what's in this for me. Once that happens I lose my focus. It's real easy to stop trying to figure out what the Father's will is.
>
> On the other hand, If I can be real open and say "I've only got a limited amount of time here. What do you want me to do? what am I here for?" that's a lot better place to be coming from.

> If you want to know God, you want to be like God, then you have to find God . . . that's a lifetime search . . . You have to be persistent because if you're not, you're not going to reach the goal. If you don't have the goal focused firmly in your mind and you keep on moving in that direction with your thoughts and actions, with your whole being, you'll lose it. You won't reach it unless you really want it. That's the same with almost anything that is worth having. Perhaps even finding a relationship.

All that's needed is your sincerity in seeking the truth and a faithful continuous effort to find God. This seeking of

God within yourself and in others is a grasp of faith that goes beyond the mind, that *must* go beyond the mind, a journey to insights and experiences of and with God. Your mind could never explain them but may acknowledge them.

> *Ask, and it will be given you; seek, and you will find; knock, and it will be opened to you. For every one who asks receives, and he who seeks finds, and to him who knocks it will be opened.*
>
> *The Bible*

Is dinner ready? Can I go now? Are we done yet? Are you ready? Where is that proposal? Why are you five minutes late? I wish that letter would get here! Pancakes take too long to make. Can't I pick the car up at 1:00 p.m.? Will it take time? Yes. Will it take a lot of effort? Yes. Do we have to be brave? Yes. Are we impatient and a little lazy, and somewhat fearful? Yes!

It's only natural that people with bodies that learned to survive through laziness and fear would frequently have animal feelings like these. The spiritual journey is the antithesis of instant gratification and will require a transcendence of mind. We must be as patient and persistent as plants growing through concrete.

If you listen, you'll hear. If you follow the leading and yield, you'll make it, at the right time, the best time, God's time.

There are four general ways to love God: We can talk to God. We can worship God. We can follow His leading; do His will. We can serve others. While these activities should be spontaneous and from your heart, it takes hard work and courage to follow your higher self. Let's explore these methods and appreciate how they work together.

Even more than our bodies need food, our spiritual development depends on these habits.

Talk to God. Mostly when friends get together, they talk, and they talk, and they talk some more, after which they talk. And so it goes. Doesn't it make sense our Father enjoys listening to us and trying to get through? Spend some time with God and speak to Him, your best friend; pour your heart out. Laugh, play, share, ask for help, ask for guidance. Most importantly, settle and listen. You'll be amazed and astounded at the satisfaction and joy of this activity.

I recall times I've spoken to God about my problems and joy. When I first started to talk to God, I wasn't sure what would happen, but as time passed I began to observe marked improvements in my mind and life. Gradually I relished my moments alone with the Creator. Whether by a serene mountain stream or in my room, I delight in speaking with God.

Worship. God is in you every moment. Share what you're thankful for and then worship God. When we worship it's our purpose to completely forget our needs and desires, to lose ourselves in a forgetful embrace of God. We do this by simply telling God how much we appreciate Him and what He's done for us and completely *avoiding any thoughts or requests for ourselves or others.* The purpose of worship is to envelop ourselves in God's presence, find out what we can do for Him, and experience eternal insights and visions to illuminate our future destiny.

Worship is unique and different from prayer and other spiritual activity. Worship is the culmination of relaxation, prayer, and thanksgiving, and is a climax of contact. God delights in touching us as we delight in His touch. Worship is our first duty and most exalted privilege and is the eternal refreshment for our happy and hungry souls.

Following God's leading. Sometimes (Do you ever do this?) I catch myself believing I know what's best for myself in the universe scheme, God's plan. Who am I kidding! I, as much as anyone, need to listen daily to God's leading and advice. All of us need to find what God wants us to do or the way we should act. In every moment God leads us to do His will: This should be our only purpose in life. Now, this may sound like we're a pile of machines to be controlled, but God wants us to do what's best for ourselves and others. It's usually later, after we look back, that we say "I guess that was what I should have done." Trust that God knows what He's doing.

For our planet's history, humans have embraced countless over-complicated and painful contortions to find God's leading. I suppose they found it hard to comprehend the simplicity of just being sincere and acting faithfully. Despite this legacy, finding the leading is simple and possible on a daily and moment by moment basis. The same way you know God exists is the same way you know what God wants you to do. You can't figure it out, but you can know it's true *without* thinking about it.

By accepting the leading and acting on it, you display that faith which will propel you into a future of glory and bring enduring spiritual success and unending satisfaction. Again, get alone, relax, pour your heart out, and listen to what God is trying to tell you.

Of course, if we ignore God, we've closed our minds. If we keep this up long enough, we'll lose our ability to know God; we will have destroyed ourselves forever; we will not exist after death, especially if we willingly hurt others: There are people who delight in using and destroying people and things. This journey is not forced on or given to anyone. You must want it and deserve it by your sincere striving for good.

Every time we're led to make a moral choice we experience divinity. When we chose to act for the benefit of others, or are willing to forego a pleasure or privilege, we're acting in a moral way. When we do what we know we should, God finds a greater home in our hearts. The Spirit is always trying to speak to you. While you still have a desire to do God's will the path will always be open. If you're sincere in your search, your internal revelation will never end.

Serving others. Loving others means we do something they want done that will help them grow spiritually or meet basic needs. This is service. The service technique changes with each situation and person because that which helps someone changes through time and with each individual. Only by listening to God do we discover the best service methods and opportunities.

The more you understand yourself and the value of others, the more you'll desire to know God. Get to know others and revel in their humanity and you'll want God more. Loving others allows us to receive 'God's love fully since we're channels opening our minds through giving; we have the right attitude. Service is the culmination of God's love for us which leads back again to God, the beginning of the love circle.

If you have God-consciousness, you're surely growing. The ideal of human life is continual progress and development as a spiritual daughter or son of the Father. God consciousness results from the experience of the personal religion you've developed, and therefore must everyone come to this point to know God better. You must decide for yourself what it is you believe.

The Benefits and Results of God-Consciousness

Again, I'm at a loss to portray the glorious, fantastic future God has in store for you. How can I describe something that's beyond our present experience and language? In trying to give you a taste I can say that knowing God and living the spiritual life will bring you **the best!!!**

The possibilities are unequivocally endless. Just think! An actual piece of God lives in you and daily shows the way. God is on your side. What limits could there be? If you do all you can, God will make you more than you are!

The experience of the heavenly Father is endless and unlimited. The possibilities and joys of your relationship with God are majestic, outstretched, glorious, enjoyable, noble, and ideal. The love of God helps us achieve these high levels of living *here and now*, not only after death. When we experience God, we should immediately strive to emulate Him, knowing He brings that perfect peace of soul and mind with resulting spirit fruits.

These people realize the significance of knowing God:

> To know my relationship with God is unlimited, first of all, tells me that this is kind of like the first step on a long long road. It tells me that experiences that I have in this life vary in importance . . . some of them are important because I will carry them forever . . . and it puts in perspective this brief time we spend on this world in terms of "What are we going to do next?"

> If I have some sort of career that spans a long, long time frame, it keeps me from being so anxious about my own well-being. It helps me to be more focused on other people; it makes me less fearful for my own personal safety; I'm more worried about doing the right thing than I am taking care of myself.

> What's the right thing to do in light of the fact that this is just the first step in a long, long, journey? And that's quite different than a lot of other people that think you have to get as much out of this life as you can possibly get out of it 'cause this is all there is. If I really believed this is all there was, I might be a whole lot more hedonistic about things. And I think that's probably the trouble with most people in the United States at this time.

> People, I think, pay lip service to the fact that there's a heaven . . . I'm not sure they really believe that, really down deep do they believe it.

> I get a great deal of comfort from that, a great deal of peace. In this world it seems that time is the enemy, that we never have enough of it, that it's always working against us, that we're always trying to beat the

clock, but in reality we have plenty of time to experience everything we want to experience.

You know the old saying "You only go around once", and "This is all you get," that's just not *true*! What you truly want to experience, what you're truly passionate about, there's plenty of time to experience it, if not in this life, then the next life.

God's not in any hurry. He's the infinite being, no beginning and no end. He doesn't judge things in terms of time. So, He'll let me take as much time as I need to do what He has in mind for me. I can't choose the curriculum, but I can choose the time it takes me to do it.

In addition, when you experience God, you gradually develop a belief in God and a knowledge of the truth. What a perfect gift! what a matchless present! God lets us know we're His children destined for greatness today, tomorrow, and forever. When we experience God, we're *given* the desire to serve others, the blessing of helping our brothers and sisters find God.

When you love your neighbor as yourself, you've realized the love of God. You see, you've allowed God to come in your life and transform your soul to new levels born of your sincerity and faith. Your God-knowing life of loving service should challenge others who've not experienced the joy of the Father. Indeed, to lead others to God is the best thing you can do.

> For though I be free from all men, yet have I made myself servant unto all, that I might gain the more.
>
> *The Bible*

If you're still unsure you're experiencing God, there are a few things to remember, a few things to look for to discover whether you've found God and how well you're progressing. But, while we're curious about our growth, *the point is to always reach out and help others* in selflessness, not to be glued to a table of introspection and an unrealistic growth schedule.

To repeat, if you have a desire to find God, you've already experienced Him. There's been a positive experience of God that's created this desire. Furthermore, the more you desire to rest with God in prayer and worship, the closer you've come to Him and will come to Him. This is the beginning of the process of eternity which will take effort and courage to continue it to know God more.

When you desire what God desires for you, you're beginning to do the will of God and deepening your intimacy with Him. There's a desire, an inexorable joy in doing the Father's will and triumphing over the old self. Also, when you begin to form your own spiritual values and recognize them, you're experiencing God more. Living a good life of love and service in partnership with God's plan shows you know God.

Since God is the source of everything, knowing Him is a process that integrates you with the universe. You'll understand the world better and desire a greater understanding of it as you progress in God experience and see your part in the beautiful cosmic design. The centerpiece of your curiosity will be God and the adventure of exploring all other relationships because these bring all life's values and real pleasures to your hungry heart.

I think a lot's been said that's confusing about religion. Ultimately, religion is a personal matter and must be tailored to you, even if you subscribe to a belief system. Certain things change, but knowing God as your Father and others as brothers and sisters is eternal since we'll progress together in the mutual experience of knowing God and doing His will. At the bottom of everyone's religion will eventually be the profound conviction that we're in this together to do God's will. This is a universal truth—the purpose of life—and it will surmount all religious prejudice, rivalry, and fear. It is The Universal Religion.

We're all His children.

Try to remember, that above all, the most important thing you can be doing is getting to know God. Everything else is a means to this end. The priority must be God; the emphasis must be God; the time and effort must be to do the will of God; all must work for cooperation with God. It's time to come to God and make the sacrifices necessary for our relationship with Him. In so doing, we'll find that this is the best life we could want.

Can you feel the joy starting? Isn't your mind beginning to expand? Do you know what's about to happen? Isn't it exciting and thrilling what awaits you? What a sublime adventure! Nothing can stop you now! Touch God! Feel God! Know God! Talk to God! Live with God! Love God! Go ahead!

Spiritual Truths

Our heavenly Father is knowable as a person.

God is the greatest experience.

Our purpose is to have a relationship with
our Universal Father.

Sincerity, faith, and effort in doing our
Fathers's will are the keys to knowing Him.

The rewards of a relationship with our
Father are perfect, unlimited, and endless.

The Family of God

The People Around You
Chapter 6

O

Recently I saw the 1960 movie *Bells Are Ringing* with Dean Martin and Judy Holliday. In one scene they stood in the middle of a crosswalk in New York City, waiting with others for the light to change, and at this point Judy began to introduce herself and say "hello" to strangers. Soon everyone in the street was speaking to one another and having a great time. Dean was surprised, but Judy wasn't; she knew the innate link in all of us that can overcome fear and prejudice; she knew that we're brothers and sisters in the Father's universe family.

The Basics and Nature of God's Family
Anywhere you go, everyone is related to you by the touch of God and physical evolution. Each person is connected because they're part of the Creator's family, kin in the deepest sense and most *literal* meaning. The Universal Father is head of this vast and varied family.

As in any ideal family, God loves each daughter or son as an *individual*. Consequently, we aren't forgotten, despite the size and complexity of all people throughout this limitless universe and our planet. In fact, it's God's love for each person that eventually creates the entire beautiful family, the summation and synthesis of individuals. If it weren't for God's love for each person, they wouldn't exist; the family wouldn't exist.

God's role and attitude is as an ideal Father ensuring His family's welfare. This means that every family member is unique, cared for, and *equally* loved because a wise father or mother would never show favoritism or reserve kindness from any child. Our loving perfect Creator loves as a Father, but beyond our concept of ideal parents.

Ponder the affect of this perspective on these people:

> If I'm driving down the road and somebody comes up behind me and flashes his lights, or I'm stopped at the intersection and somebody takes the right of way, or something like that, If I'm self-centered then I might go and try to fight back. But if I understand that those other people are just my brothers and my sisters, and maybe they're havin' a bad day or maybe there's an emergency or maybe there's somethin' else goin' on, then *fine*, I can be more relaxed about the whole thing.
>
> That's a daily occurrence. And I don't think it's being a wimp about the whole thing. It's just recognizing that, hey we're all on this boat together. I think it gives me a lot more compassion and empathy for the other person.

> I try to behave towards them as I perceive God would behave towards them or I would perceive Jesus would behave towards them. I try to keep in mind that although I don't know them and don't love them, *somebody* loves that person. That person has a mother and father, and maybe a wife or husband, children, people that adore that person, count on that person, depend on that person. So every time I make a connection with a person, I'm not only touching that person's life but I'm touching the lives of all of those people who love that person and know that person.

Here we can't forget the importance of God as the Creator of all people. In order to have a universe with persons and a universal family, God is absolutely essential for it's only through origin in Him that we're siblings, related offspring. It's invigorating to know we're bonded to strangers and realize our potential relationships with them are only limited by our and their decisions, not our mutual ignorance of each other.

The truth is, we only come to this insight if *we find and experience God as a Father*. It's impossible to know your fellows as brothers and sisters unless you've found God as a father since all other makeshift attempts and substitutes are a waste of time and a delusion. You must find God first.

> We love, because he first loved us. If any one says, "I love God," and hates his brother, he is a liar; for he who does not love his brother whom he has seen, cannot love God whom he has not seen. And this commandment we have from him, that he who loves God should love his brother also.
>
> *The Bible*

This ability to know God as Father and all other people as kin is a divine gift. It's a gift we overlook . . .

. . . It's quite interesting and pleasing to relate to another person. It isn't just that both of you like the same music or activities, but that a profound similarity operates between you which is revealed and released through these activities. There is an immediate recognition among you because you share the experience of being a person, and that's something only *people* can do with other people, not with pets, plants, or landscapes. That's communication, consciousness to consciousness.

While similarities are pleasing, we must address and go beyond our endless differences and work together toward a common goal—a better way of living and a better world—

because ignoring this leads to societal disintegration. Thus, we're best unified in the knowledge that each of us has a life purpose to live the Father's will and serve others. Since God has a plan for us and each of us, it only makes sense to work together to realize this plan for the best life.

Unity of individuals and nations will only occur when they work together to practice the art of doing God's will. All other unity is based on superficial similarities rather than the *real* similarity of God's Spirit within and His plan for everyone.

We're once again faced with the necessity of understanding our common spiritual origin and destiny; humankind was created by God for a spiritual destiny and must realize this to find and practice the brotherhood of man. Everyone must strive to know God and do His will. What other force could bind so many of us together? What other information can lead us to dissolve hatreds and seek an embrace? Our Father's family is based on spiritual unity, not beliefs or appearances.

I suppose the majority of us like most people, but without the common unity of God, the natural differences of race, culture, religion, and nation can and do create an attitude of separateness. We wouldn't see ourselves as related because we would look for superficial unity. Something deeper must be harnessed, something independent of physical differences or cultural beliefs.

The reaction of our animal minds is to defend and look for differences as a basis for this defense. *Our civilization is disintegrating into tiny pieces based on shallow differences.* This is happening because most people have forgotten about our God and our common spiritual nature and, therefore, petty differences rear up and confuse us, distract us.

In the universe brotherhood *all are equal*! There are no castes or classes. Our Father views people in two ways: He sees those who know Him and those who don't.

Since our family is composed of individuals, unity must start here. Eventually, the great waves of change that sweep a world begin with each person and the effect of these creates an unstoppable evolutionary force. If we want to make a new world we've got to look in the mirror and grow spiritually, strive to know God, and help each other.

I think we've relied too long on governments and organizations to live for us. How many people secretly desire to become a part of the movie they're watching or affect the world events they constantly complain about? How often do you wish you could do something? You can! You can be part of the spiritual renaissance, a pioneer in the most profound adventure the world has yet experienced.

Listen to this person's enthusiasm:

> I feel that the most important way I contribute to the spiritual renaissance is with my relationships because I feel like I put a lot of love and attention and time, deliberately put a lot of time into my relationships. I feel like I can be a living example.
>
> I really believe very strongly that the Father works on this plane through us . . . once we take that commitment seriously. So many times people say: "Well, if there is a God then why is there suffering? why is there this? why is there that? why is there pain?" It's there because God's children are allowing it to be there.
>
> We can, at any time, choose to help, and choose to alleviate that, choose to make your feelings matter. What you're feeling matters to me, and I don't want you to be sad. So, I will take whatever time I need to help you if you need my help. It doesn't mean that I would impose my help on you. But if you were to ask for my help, I would stop whatever I was doing and help you however I could. And stop at nothing to restore your self-respect. I think the most important thing we can do is to take time to help each other and not be so selfish.
>
> And that's the spiritual renaissance. The spiritual renaissance is the brotherhood of man, the realization of the brotherhood of man. And so anything I can do to

> bring that about, whether it be poetry or speaking, ya'
> know . . .

To know others as brothers and sisters means you have to make a few changes in personal relations. Think of your best friends or your closest family members. How do you treat them? Are you loving and patient? Do you seek to understand them? It may be almost second nature to do this with familiar people, but you'll have to apply this same love to every person you see and know because we're all family. Once you know God there's no getting around this fact.

This takes spirituality. It takes effort. It means growth.

Ensuring the Best for the Family

O.K. Here we are in this together with our many talents, temperaments, past experiences, and differing philosophies. How can we cooperate to make our lives better? What'll unify us? What's our central vision? What's our guidance? Undoubtedly, this unifying essence is God's goal.

God's goal is to have the greatest good for the greatest number of people for the greatest duration—eternity. God's plan embraces the unlimited stretches of stars and everyone who inhabits the planets around those stars: Everyone can participate. God loves the entire family and cares about the sum effect of our behavior. It's true God loves you, but He also loves everyone equally. This *whole* is the universe brotherhood. To achieve an ideal world we must sacrifice as a team, like any successful group. We can't get our way merely because it feels good or is easier. *Everybody* has obligations to themselves and others and must experience the consequences of mistakes and self-centeredness.

God created these consequences and constraints for the good of us *all*. If we had no rules or plan, there'd be no enjoyment, creation, or living. Working together as a group means the group has to cooperate and use rules, tolerance, patience, and compromise, without which it's destroyed. The same rules and constraints that allow us to work together as a team are the same realities that require us to become spiritual, to forgo immediate pleasures and to work hard. This is the fusion of everyone's uniqueness (differences) to make a better world and require a lot of giving. Only a life of unselfish spiritual living can achieve this kind of success.

Many times this means sacrifice, which is illustrated in this interview:

> I fell fairly madly in love with a guy who had just recently gotten divorced. I had a very intense experience of connecting, of intimacy, of communication, and of being able to share, spiritually, and I thought this was *it* . . . I found it fairly easy to incorporate him into my family plans and into my future. It was a real whirlwind experience. And it was a very beautiful experience.
>
> After a few months, he got very depressed about something one weekend and was having a hard time talking to me about it. I pulled it out of him after hours of talking. He was feeling some remorse about leaving his wife, his x-wife. And feeling like he wasn't going to be able to have a full-fledged relationship with his kids. He had just spent the weekend with them and had had a wonderful experience with them.
>
> After hearing him talk about it I thought "Well, those all sound really legitimate. If you think that you made a big mistake, maybe it's not too late. Maybe you can go back; maybe she would forgive you; maybe you could reconcile." He was like "No. No. No. I think that would be impossible. I'm not ready to make a decision like that. This is something I'm thinking of off in the future maybe a year from now, maybe two years from now."
>
> And I immediately got very adamant. "Look! If this is something you think you may be able to do, you can't wait; you have to do it now. She may not be available a year from now." And I got real committed to this family. And I said "I really think the family is the most important thing you can experience in this lifetime. And being a good father is more important than any other job you will

> ever have. This has eternal ramifications. What you do for a living is really not that relevant. This is where your commitment lies."
>
> It feels like one of the most selfless things I've seen myself doing. It was very painful because *I* wanted him. It was something I knew was right. It was something I knew I was doing for the benefit of the group of that family and of our society as a whole . . . Even though it was painful, it wasn't hard at all. There was no doubt in my mind. It was a clear road of God's will. There wasn't any hesitation. It was interesting because the pain of the heartbreak dissipated fairly quickly for me and was replaced by a renewed commitment to family as a whole.

God acts for the benefit of the whole, not one individual. While God's mandates are designed for the best outcome for everyone, He shows mercy to each of us. This doesn't mean He'll change the way things run, but that He'll give you another chance if you're sincere. God's relation to the universe and its individuals is determined by His will.

God's will is always shown in the way the whole of humanity is progressing, indeed, the *whole* of persons in the universe. I can fail to listen to God and go my selfish way (Many others can also.), but most people deeply desire to know their Creator-Father and are moving in the direction He wants them to. Most of the world is slowly progressing towards the realization of a better civilization and a better individual life.

I taught elementary school for years as a substitute and regular teacher, my classes varied in size and ability, in cooperativeness and friendliness, but they were basically fine. These children wanted to learn and were enjoyable to teach; they were helpful and hardworking. I bent the rules sometimes as long as it didn't hurt the class and helped the individual. I think the universe is a little like my classes were with its components of mercy and law, designed for the good of all.

In the beginning God wished to render justice, but when He observed that the world could not rest on justice alone, He rendered mercy.

The Talmud

Just like my classes though, one person always affects the lives of many, many others. In life we're pleased by someone who helps others and is good and we're glad he or she affects a wide range of people. While the benefits of a person motivated and centered on serving others are manifold, the converse is also true of those obsessed with self-gratification and destruction, borne out by crime, disrespect, and grave mistakes. Since God allows us to act unrestricted, we *always* affect many people independent of their say in the matter.

The reason we must experience others' actions is simple: For people to have freewill, they must be allowed to make decisions. And, when we live in a world of immaturity and confusion, people are bound to make mistakes and act selfishly from time to time. It's only by allowing this freewill that God can give growth and the gift of a universe family. Otherwise we'd be machines.

Anyone knows this makes life painful and challenging. Mistakes and willful cruelty have always affected and sometimes destroyed the lives of others. Millions have died and suffered the destruction and abuse of their bodies by aggressors or have experienced mental abuse or other limitations. We can't deny this! But, **nothing can harm your spiritual progress and real happiness!** You can live forever and know God because you have freewill. For the most part, though, we're working together and things are getting better. As bleak as our current civilization appears, we should have patience and courage to bridge the uncivilized swamp.

Living as a Family

How do we do it? What can we do to work in unison for the will of the Creator? It's necessary for everyone to help if we want to progress at the best rate. To act as a spiritual brotherhood, what ingredients do we need? It all comes down to this: How do each of us learn to experience and *live* brotherhood?

Who among us wouldn't give all for a friend or family member? I think the great majority of us would probably give our lives for a dear friend, a child, or a spouse, because we love them and desire the best for them; we want to do everything in our power to "make it happen." In addition, I think our greatest pleasures and satisfactions take place during such service: The heights and ideals of human relationships are attained in the joyful act of serving, doing something a person wants done for them, something that will help them.

Serving someone is the secret of experiencing brotherhood with family, friends, and others. You may understand and agree that humanity should be unified through spirituality, you may see all as brothers and sisters, but your heart won't *feel* it until you respond to your service desires. Brotherhood begins when we treat others as we wish to be treated and as we believe God would treat us.

Brotherhood manifests in a twofold way. First, we begin to have an inner experience and certainty that all people are unified through God and are kin—brotherhood feelings. Then tangible results begin to form from our acts of service and the world around us (at least the part we can affect) begins to improve. These two parts of the family experience form an unending cycle, from feelings of brotherhood and inspiration toward real results which give rise to *more* feelings of brotherhood which begin the process again, repeatedly.

> *A person completely wrapped up in himself makes a small package . . . The great day comes when a man begins to get himself off his hands. He has lived, let us say, in a mind like a room surrounded by mirrors. Every way he turned he saw himself. Now, however, some of the mirrors change to windows. He can see through them to objective outlooks that challenge his interests. He begins to get out of himself—no longer the prisoner of self-reflections but a free man in a world where persons, causes, truths, and values exist, worthful for their own sakes. Thus to pass from a mirror-mind to a mind with windows is an essential element in the development of a real personality. Without that experience no one ever achieves a meaningful life.*
>
> Harry Emerson Fosdick

The very basis of human fellowship is the drive and desire for social service. It's the *religious* person who goes out and engages in this service with the attitude of unselfish love, conscious of partnership with God.. When you have this attitude of God, you're willing to do all things necessary for the progress and well-being of your brother or sister no matter what the cost.

When you become conscious that you're part of the family of God, you appreciate the numerous gifts you've been given. It's out of this thankfulness that service arises. Service is required to become an active family member who is well integrated and living the rule of the family. This rule informs us it's our responsibility to serve other family members when we realize we're a part of the family.

Observe this person's channel of service:

> There's an organization here in town called an incubator. And what it does is it helps small fledgling companies get going, and nurtures them. I have been spending a lot of time on that since the first of the year without any compensation or anything like that, spend

ing a lot of time and effort and so on. Because, the organization is really *struggling* right now.

I've been getting a lot of flack from my wife, "Well, why don't you do something that pays some money?" And it's kind of like "No, what I'm doing is important and it's something I have to do because it's a not-for-profit, service organization. And I'm really helping to go make things better there." And so, that sacrifice feels right. And even though other people are kind of saying "What are you getting involved with that thing for?" I know it's the right thing to do so I just go do it.

And after that's over with it just feels like "O.K., that's what you want me to do . . . go do it." There's a sense of harmony . . . One of the things I discovered out on the Indian Reservation was this concept of harmony. They happen to believe in harmony with the earth, harmony with each other. They're a whole lot better at it, quite frankly, than mainstream U.S. society.

When I go and make a sacrifice and really start lookin' out for the other person, I finally begin to feel this sense of harmony and that we really are one. We are brothers and sisters. I'm just doin' my part . . . We have something we can learn there from them because it's so basic. They aren't nearly as "me oriented" or "I oriented" as the rest of our society is.

When you serve your sisters and brothers, you're then able to feel God's love.

Before, I mentioned a cycle of inspiration and action, but there is, of course, another cycle. When I receive the Father's love I'm thrilled and invigorated by serving others and I've *enlarged* my capacity and receptivity to experience God. In addition, the same happens in those I serve since they're affected and experience a little of God through my actions. Consequently, they're also led to perform the very acts of service I gave them which then inspire others to do the same. All of us are united in helping each other grow because God is helping us grow. Everyone ends up striving together if they're united through a common spiritual experience.

God's Family and Our Civilization

Just imagine the expansive possibilities of service—living the principles of brotherhood. The transformations in our society will be astounding. If enough people live these ways, what limits can be placed on our progress? The mighty seed will root and flourish, spreading everywhere. The ideal and experience of knowing God as Father and others as family is the *greatest* truth the world we will know, and when humankind rediscovers this unlimited family relationship, civilization will transform through uplifting service.

Politicians and social scientists try to define the best ingredients of a nation, but the ideal state is based on the fatherhood of God and the brotherhood of man. The love generated by this brotherhood will give us the power to solve every plaguing problem and thrust us forward. When nations have citizens who love unselfishly, when people realize they're children of the Creator and are family, we'll realize the brotherhood of man, the brightest civilization.

But, with this idealism let's not forget common sense and reasoning. While I want to serve my fellows, I know I must simultaneously insure that the will of the group, the will of the family, is carried out, achieving the best for all. The selfish actions of another mustn't be allowed if they go against the group will and make things hard for everyone. If the people of a community or a country want to do things in a certain way, why in the world should they allow a person or a small group to halt their plans as long as their choices are *fair* to all groups? Doesn't the majority have the right to strive for a fair and just world? This means that the new brotherhood must protect itself.

Countries won't find peace within their borders or between themselves until they're unified through a belief and dedication to the fatherhood of God and the brotherhood of man. This means they must be willing to *protect* their

citizens from the cruel acts of selfish people and the problems of materialistic or totalitarian governments.

Our civilization is a ship at sea with few willing to pump
out water, steer a course, raise sail, or feed the crew. This
lack of brotherly love can and does produce anger which
leads only to more stubbornness and unreasonableness and
blocks creation of the brotherhood of man. In today's local
and world climate, only brotherhood can prevent the strong
and powerful from oppressing the weak and the powerless.
Only brotherhood can set us on the right course to a horizon
of spiritual discovery, progress, and fairness.

Further, another disturbing process compounds the
problem: the formation of "US" groups. Let's say someone
experiences frustration or injustice. He next attributes it to
the natural superficial differences (race, religion, nationality,
etc.) between himself and the offender and reasons it's the
differences that caused the injustice or frustration more than
the character problems or selfishness of the offender.

With this assumption (prejudice) the abused person forms
a group that shares his religion, race, nationality, etc., and
attacks people who are similar to his offender in nationality,
race, religion, etc. The real cause of the original problem is
drowned in a cacophony of prejudice and fear. The same
happens on the other side. Therefore, each side won't listen
to reason because they believe the problem comes from
superficial *differences* between their groups much more than
the choices and mistakes of the people who caused the
original problem. This is the US/THEM syndrome and it's as
old as our species and as natural as breathing.

However, as sorry as this scene is, we can exit. If we see
ourselves as God's daughters and sons we'll be unified in one
US through the most significant similarity and transcend the
divisive similarities we use to separate each other with—religion, race, nationality, etc. This is the *only* way to bridge
the gap of real human differences. We must get together to

celebrate the sameness of God in our lives and the unity of our task.

If we do this, what will happen to our lives, our home-towns, our countries, our world-civilization?

When we engage the immensity of brotherhood, this earth will see an unprecedented era of social wisdom and cooperation. We'll do what's right and harmoniously solve problems by addressing their causes, by understanding each other, and unifying through mutual love born of *spiritual experience*. The planet will head to unlimited progress derived from a spiritual civilization dedicated to service and God.

> You should be made all the better citizens of the secular government as a result of becoming enlightened sons of the kingdom; so should the rulers of earthly governments become all the better rulers in civil affairs as a result of believing this gospel of the heavenly kingdom. The attitude of unselfish service of man and intelligent worship of God should make all kingdom believers better world citizens, while the attitude of honest citizenship and sincere devotion to one's temporal duty should help to make such a citizen the more easily reached by the spirit call to sonship in the heavenly kingdom.
>
> The Urantia Book

This is the group picture, but how about your life? What will it do for every person? Well, because you'll know God personally you'll be supremely loyal to his plan, committed to service no matter the cost. You'll understand that ultimately this is the best future for you and others, doing the Father's will without restriction or limitation.

Frequently we think about the benefits and deprivations of a decision, as if doing right was mathematics. It's only when we realize we're members of God's family that we know cooperation with God benefits us. This is the genesis of our loyalty to the ideal of service.

Your social activities and personal interactions will take on new vitality. Everyone will sense you're a true friend and a loving associate through thick and thin. Graciousness and sensitivity will pervade every action, tactfulness the badge of every communication. You'll be part of the emerging civilization of the brotherhood of man.

If you know God as a Father, you know every human being as a sibling. Look around, wherever you are, at home, outside, at work. Each and every person is your sister or brother, a new adventure in service to be discovered and a new server to help you. Talk about networking! The world is your network! It's your ever-present opportunity to experience love, trust, and challenge.

This person provides a clear illustration:

> Habitat For Humanity is a group that's running fairly strongly throughout the world. It's people helping other people help themselves. And it seems like a very progressive service organization. They build homes. They started, I think, in the anchor city here in the States, in the very poor South. They've developed a network of volunteers as well as some minimally paid positions all over the world. It's spreading very rapidly.
>
> Basically they build a home, usually in the neighborhood of about twenty-five to thirty-thousand dollars because they have a lot of the materials donated. The family whose home is being built for them has to commit x number of hours worth of labor to building a home for the next family. They usually invest in building the home they're gonna live in also.
>
> It's a real labor of love, of community coming together and producing something that's really necessary for poor people. But it's not like most charities that are giving something for nothing and then developing a dependency. I see them as really promoting a sense of accomplishment for the people *themselves*. Because they're learning skills and doing something important for

themselves and for other people, they start to develop a sense of purpose and confidence and self-esteem. It's ecumenical, a real positive thing.

Remember that person this week or the week before who hurt you or made you angry? Can you see the face? Can you hear the words? No matter what happened, this person is your kin: Your *obligation* and *responsibility* is to serve them the best way you know. Only through understanding them and letting God's love through can you do this. That is why the Fatherhood of God is so important. This is your challenge.

And as you have a responsibility to others they have one to you! Trust the guidance and leadings of the Spirit of God and you'll find all you need through the assistance of others. You're always at home, never alone, although life can hurt so badly and be so confusing that you want to isolate yourself. But this shouldn't last. Go to your family in trust and act with faith. God will bring someone to serve you. That's what family is for.

"Ya gotta have friends." Be thrilled! Be encouraged! Be comforted! Be invigorated! Be electrified! Be strengthened! Not only are you a child of God, but so is everyone, all growing together. We're people and can communicate and have the Spirit of the Father in us. Is there a better life than this? We're here together to know the deepest joy, the most supreme spiritual achievement possible—service to each other. We need each other. **We are family!**

Make every day a reunion. Reach out with soft hand and bright smile. Listen with attentive ear and understanding mind and give all you are; go the second mile. Make a new friend; serve an old one. Touch a child of God.

Spiritual Truths

God is everyone's Father.

We are all brothers and sisters.

Our purpose is to do our Father's will
together—to serve each other.

Our world is destined to become a paradise.

To achieve progress together, we must serve
and sacrifice unselfishly and joyously.

The Spirit God

Your Guide, Your Companion
Chapter 7

O

If you were ever lost in a store as a child, you remember the anxiety, and later the relief. Usually, you were out with your parents and just got sidetracked and distracted by a new toy or display. In reality, you were never in danger because your parents were close by all the time.

While we're grownups now, our lives mirror this common experience when we feel alone, afraid, and depressed in daily responsibilities and complications. However, *inside* each of us there lives a Spirit of God, awaiting opportunities to enlighten our minds, energize our actions, and uplift our souls. Everyone is filled with our Father's **absolute** love through the work of these individual Spirits. There could be no greater gift, for with these guides all things are possible in spiritual progress! We can live a successful spiritual life here and continue the adventure after death in an eternity of growth.

We Need Help!
O.K. Let's be honest and realistic about our lives; let's admit our faults and failings and *examine* (no small task) our

situation. We must be willing to accept the cause of our dissatisfactions and ascertain the essentials of goal realization, instead of pleasure stimulation and work avoidance. This is the surest way to work out problems and improve our lives. Let's do what's necessary to live the ideal life, our ideal vision. Everything else is a mere avoidance game.

The first blunt fact is that we're humans born from aeons of evolutionary survival struggles and pleasure pursuits. This evolutionary process is doubly our collective genesis and the root of personal change, ever challenging us to adapt, survive, and grow. While we have little control over physical potentials, *we* can determine personal and societal changes. This is God's plan—slow, gradual change.

There are many things facing you and me as evolutionary creatures. Foremost, we need to survive by meeting our material and social needs while protecting ourselves. Further, we also have dynamic desires to achieve goals and our dreams. And adding to this personal mix are the pitfalls and dangers of pride, unbalanced living, selfishness, fear, and laziness which we must monitor and be saved from.

And superimposed on this evolutionary foundation is our yearning to be better, to become that ideal person we visualize. In addition to this vision, there is another, our picture of a perfect world. Talk to any child under ten; she's filled with an ideal vision of herself and the world and is determined to achieve them. This common experience reveals that most people want to be happy and are working toward this end.

Can you feel the yearnings deep in your heart and the needs in your mind? Are you conscious of your dreams of a better life, the things you would like to become and do? Do you know how to nourish your spiritual self as well as your material? Our loving Creator-Father purposefully plants these desires, not to torment and taunt us but to invigorate us to

achieve the eternal life which satisfies these endless and
infinite motivations.

No one can ignore his or her yearnings or leave personal
needs unfulfilled and expect happiness. It would be like
taking a seed and expecting growth without soil, water, or
sun. Yet, people do this constantly. It's clear we can't meet
our needs or overcome problems alone; we need other people
and God because we don't have enough power or insights.
*The only answer to individual and social problems is the
spiritual life.*

Here's one person's view on these urges:

> Human perfection-hunger, for me, has always been
> perceived in my life as trying to do the most amount of
> good for the most amount of people for the longest
> amount of time. As a result, this has become a philoso-
> phy of living for me.
>
> Short-term gains at long-term expense has never
> made any sense to me in any way, shape, or form. I
> sense that a tremendous amount of this type of thinking
> comes from the Spirit within: I've always been con-
> nected to it; I've never been totally satisfied with the
> norm of how things are done; I've always thought that
> things could be a tremendous amount different than the
> way they are here on this planet right now.
>
> Every time somebody has looked down their long
> dark nose at me and said, "Because that's the way it is."
> My response has always been, "No. That's the way it is
> *here* now. They're other possibilities."

The result of these yearnings is an effort to be happy.
Therefore, everyone goes out and tries to be happy. We try
to affect our lives, and then everyone else's, believing our
way is perfect, best for all. We simply try to solve our
problems and reach our goals in the way **we** think is best.
*Most of the time we don't compromise but simply look out for
ourselves because we're selfish or believe we're right.* This is

nothing new, considering our evolutionary heritage. There is an evolutionary code that's easy to slip into.

> *To put it briefly, there are two widespread human characteristics which are responsible for the fact that the regulations of civilization can only be maintained by a certain degree of coercion—namely, that men are not spontaneously fond of work and that arguments are of no avail against their passions.*
>
> Sigmund Freud

The common first step is to concentrate our energies to get what we need and then protect ourselves so nothing interferes with or endangers our acquisitions. And since it's better to save ourselves (to conserve energies) we choose to avoid all effort aside from meeting needs and self-defense. This leads to one result: We stay the same and resist all change or challenge. We do this because material evolution patiently taught us these rules of survival. After all, it has always worked.

Thus, the hallmark of our animal minds is *sloth* and *fear*. These evolutionary tendencies helped us survive, but now give rise to gnawing unhappiness, continued dissatisfaction, debilitating depression, and endless conflicts. Is it any wonder so many people have conflicts since they're only looking out for themselves? What life can we expect for ourselves and humankind if we live only by evolutionary survival tendencies?

Despite these evolutionary tendencies, we can make spiritual choices and use instincts as opportunities for transformation.

The Spirit of God

While it's a fact that God designs our evolutionary birth, He also provides transcendence of this animal life. You and *everyone who desires one* has a personal guide and helper, the Spirit of God. We get one when we make our first moral choice. The only requirement for receiving a personal Spirit is intention, *not belief.* This is your light, your salvation, a personal Gift from God the Father.

The most instructive way to view and relate to this Spirit is as an ideal friend. This being is beyond your imagination, perfect in every way and your understanding teacher and guide. You're in the school of life and you've got a private teacher *for free* and can get help with every problem, vanquish every fear, and help any person.

This Spirit of God comes right from the Father. Your inner friend is a **direct link** to the universe Creator and is better than any phone or other communications system because this friend lives in you. If you need inspiration, energy for work, or any *quality,* God will bring it through this friend. Your associate can transform your mind and soul to majestic heights of spiritual living and valleys of tranquility. This inner Spirit is the closest link God has with any part of His creation, and you've got it.

Your personal individual guide is a being once a part of God but who's chosen to reside with you to help you grow. You might think of your Spirit of God as a perfect being who's a "chip off the old block." Reassuringly, everyone has his or her own individual Spirit of God.

This Spirit is our only proof of the Father's existence, the greatest evidence of His love and goodness, and the highest reason for falling in love with Him. We're created in God's image through the gift of these individual Spirit guides and He gives us everything we'll ever need through these Spirits.

> I've always felt in contact with something other than myself. I've been told that it was many things at different points in my life, depending on who was telling me what: I've been told it was my guardian angel. I've been told miscellaneous things about this inner voice, but I've always been conscious of it. And I've often

sensed that maybe a number of other people that were around me were either not hearing it, not listening to it, or not getting it. People say they beat a different drum. That's the way I've always felt.

It is very comforting to me because I sense that I'm on the right path as a result of being in connection with that voice. The idea that it's just as joyful about its experience with me as I am with it is a real comforting thought to me. The idea that it really *means* something to some other being or entity when I succeed or when I fail at something is *good*, it gives me somebody to look up to that's above and beyond what we have here on this planet to deal with.

We're dealing with a lot of societal veils here. We've got religions, politics, big business . . . more than willing to throw all kinds of wool blankets over our eyes all the time. It is nice to feel that I have a connection with some level of intelligence that is *objective* to all of that.

So, what is this Spirit teacher like? What can you expect from such an intimate partner? Most importantly, this friend is a real piece of God. God chooses to live in us by taking these Spirits and placing them inside our minds to portray and live His attitude and will. Your internal guide is pure spirit and energy since it came from God. There are no limits.

The Spirit's behavior is the way of God. Firstly, your friend is absolutely dedicated to improving your spiritual progress and revealing God eternally: *Your friend will be with you forever, never to abandon you.* That's stunning. No matter what you do, think, or say, this friend will be with you and help you as long as you still desire God. There are "no strings attached" to its help.

The Spirit also knows the challenge. Because we're evolutionary creatures, things take a *long* time. We start out with nothing and gradually make decisions that create spiritual selves and eternal futures as slowly as water goes to the ocean. The Spirit in your mind knows this and will be with you always and be patient always. This Spirit consummately loves you beyond degree and doesn't quit.

> The (Spirits) are loving leaders, your safe and sure guides through the dark and uncertain mazes of your short earthly career; they are patient teachers who so constantly urge their subjects forward in the paths of progressive perfection. They are the careful custodians of the sublime values of creature character. I wish you could love them more, co-operate with them more fully, and cherish them more affectionately.

> *The Urantia Book*

Of course, problems arise in this spiritualizing process. To surmount these, your Spirit must be strong, industrious, and tenacious (as must you). I suppose trying to spiritualize us is like trying to dig a mountain tunnel with a toothpick. For this Spirit to stay with you through every setback and triumph it must have endless endurance, for it never stops its work!

The Spirit's behavior is perfect. This friend acts ideally with a perfect attitude and always represents God the Father. This friend **never** makes a mistake or in any way endangers your spiritual destiny. It's difficult to visualize this, but, when faced with our problems and behavior, it's plain this is necessary.

Our Spirit guides give us everything. How do we know God? How do we see the spiritual? It's by the work of our inner friends. The Father's unlimited and powerful love embraces us through the work of these Spirits in our minds. God is willing to do everything He can for us and is willing to wait as long as it takes. Our Spirit guides *are* the Father's love, the perfect representatives of the divine affection.

Also, how can we know truth, know when something is spiritually true? Again, it's through the unending toil of these gems that you and I can know God, find His will, discern what's spiritually true, and have a desire to know others. By showing us spirit living, our teachers purify our thinking and activate our living. These friends show us the truth.

To understand the significance of the Spirit, let's think of intimacy. The best way to get close to someone is to help and listen to them. When the expression is true to the friendship or relationship, we're physically close, whether it be a pat on the back, a hug, or sexual contact. As rewarding as this is, we must remember God has *far* more intimate contact with us because He lives at the very root of our being. At the core He lives with you during every moment, every thought. Your most important and intimate relationship is with God through the work of His Spirit.

The Spirit's Mission and Techniques

There is one point to life—to live in a spiritual way and become like God, to be happy. The Spirit is here to represent God so you can become spiritual and know the Father. In fact, this is all the Spirit is concerned with.

This priority of spiritualizing you never changes, but what does change is our responses to the perfect work of our individual Spirits. Usually we get involved with only making a living and surviving—that same old animal logic and pattern. We've all done and continue to do it, but our Spirits yearn for us to wake up to the purpose of these challenges and afflictions. The rent, the insult, failing health, a troubled country, all these never affect your real spiritual progress, but instead can be a boon to growth.

Yes, I agree, life can be painful and very cruel, but the purpose of pain and unhappiness is to cause spiritual growth, *period*. While these troubles aren't punishments or signs from God, they can become the stimulus to discover His signs and love within. Everything should work to this end. And so, when you look at the frustrations and injustices of the present, remember these won't harm your spiritual self. In the end, everything is left behind; at death, only your spiritual self goes with you with your memories and self-consciousness.

I think we can learn something about life after death from this person:

> Thank goodness my good memories are going to be there because I would hate to start out all over again and not have any memory of anything. Then it would be as if I had never lived before. It would make this life somewhat meaningless if I was not able to take anything from this life. These memories are going to be very, very important in maintaining who I am throughout eternity.
>
> Without the memories I would be impersonal; I would not have the basis for why the personality is the way it is without memories of love, without memories of pain, without memories of how you got to be where you are now. Without that, you're like a person with no experience at all. Just all of a sudden you're resurrected in a body (Imagine that.). And you're there and you're like "Oh. Who am I?" And then they tell you. "Well, where did I come from?" "Well, you lived on earth." They would give you everything without any actual personal recollection.
>
> Without those memories, it makes this life meaningless. It would be as if you had not experienced it at all. It wouldn't make any sense.

Consequently, your Spirit is on a mission to show you God and continue to transform you with His love and energy. All this is to *help you create and continually nourish your soul.* Your soul is the spiritual part based on spiritual decisions. It's your ticket to an eternal existence and destined to be your spiritual clothing, always aiding you in life and extending your destiny. Your soul is a vehicle to the next life. Every time you choose to do the Father's will, you add to and improve this vehicle. When you die, your soul will take *you* to the afterlife.

We appreciate how spirituality improves life here, but I think most of us first want to know we live after we die. I want to keep going, to enjoy the life I've made and live with friends and make new ones; I want to travel to new places and make new discoveries; I have numerous ideas and goals that can't possibly be brought into existence on this planet or in this lifetime. I'm sure you have similar desires for a better life and adventures of achievement and unlimited exploration. Humankind shares these desires and can have them realized.

> *If we are but born into the Pure Land by embarking upon Amida's original vow, then none of our cherished desires remain unfulfilled.*
>
> Hônen

God graciously gives eternal life to let us satisfy our spiritual longings, the very longings He gives. Our Father plants and fosters these longings and visions inside to stimulate our hearts to live the better way and seek destiny with Him. God places His sweet Spirit in you to show eternal life and satisfy all spiritual ambitions that help others and yourself. *Your talents, experiences, and goals won't be wasted.* Everything you achieved here (spiritual and mindal progress) will be yours in eternal life. If you listen to the Spirit in sincerity, you'll live forever and realize every dream.

How does this pleasant companion achieve such transformations from raw evolutionary creatures like ourselves? Where does your eternal friend focus and act with nobility and love? What methods does this infinite piece of God use? Before we delve into this discussion, we must remember that *all the Spirit does for us is done only with our permission.* If in our heart of hearts we don't want change to happen, we don't want to grow, we don't want to try, then, if God is to respect our freewill, how can we be transformed? How can we be spiritualized? God can only spiritualize us if we wholeheartedly want it and work for such change.

Essentially, our spiritual guides concentrate their energies on our minds, where we visualize, plan, and act on our decisions. When your heart is engaged in a decision, your Spirit hopes your heart listens to its suggestions. This Spirit is trying to spiritualize your thoughts to lead to superhuman actions: We act as we think.

Usually we catch a distant glimpse of eternal visions or guidance. But, progress is only made if we're sincere and express our intention to have this spiritual work done. As mentioned before, this Spirit is using our minds to get through to us, to lead us to spiritual decisions that create our souls. This is the key to eternal life.

Your Spirit is a direct channel for the Father's love to you, and potentially to others through you. All the divine affection you can experience is poured on with a gentle hand, a parental caress, through the Spirit. It's the placement of this joyous Spirit that allows you to enjoy and benefit from the Creator's love.

Your Spirit begins by slowly building a foundation. First, your Spirit gives a certainty that the Father and other people exist. If it wasn't for this gift of certainty, no one would bother to have human contacts, let alone good friendships. And secondly, without the knowledge (the feeling) that God exists, life would be reduced to the blind survival struggle of an evolutionary animal. This gift of relationships is the basis for life as a human being, a social animal.

After the certainty that God and others are real, we're given the desire to know that real God. We wish with all our hearts to get closer to our Maker. Isn't it natural to want to say "thank you" to the one who's made existence possible? The Spirit within makes it possible to seek a friendship with God and stokes the desire to choose God. It's this desire to know God that gives birth to the ambition to become like Him, to be the best in our own way.

Furthermore, who could live without the activating gifts of sublime yearning and desires for personal best? Your Spirit friend brings the delicious desire and yearning to become the best. I can't imagine life without a craving to do my best. Everything I started would end in meaningless confusion or violence and the people I rely on would slip into a careless attitude and begin to act selfishly. We would be devoid of our humanity without the choice of desiring to be Godlike and doing the work of God.

Considering those around us, we know they too have the same desire for perfection. This can release the longing for service (another desire placed by the Spirit) because we recognize that others are like ourselves and hence want help to know God to satisfy their perfection hunger. If our actions help another to become perfect, *we've* taken a step to perfection and have listened to the Spirit.

This service desire is the foundation of all true friendships and successful human group interactions. It brings, along with the certainty that others are real, the birth of the brotherhood of all and the achievements of a worthy civilization. The secret of a better world is in living a better human life; it's in striving for perfection through service to others.

This person knows the nature of growth:

> It's relieving to know I'm perfecting every day. Seeing where I am now, it's nice to know that perfection is my goal, my *destiny*, it's certainly not my condition. In some things I can be a perfectionist, like trying to get a piece of wood just right for a finished product or working on a poster or something, going through so many different versions of it just to get it right. And it feels good once you get it to a place where you think really justifies the work you put into it. It's beautiful or has a positive affect when you look at it.

> To know that we're heading towards perfection . . .
> it's going to be heading towards feeling good about what
> you do and how you relate to things. I associate a sense
> of perfection with a sense of accomplishment, a sense
> of pride (somewhat), or doing a job well.

How do I do it? What am I to do? What is God's will for me? Again, if you look to the friend waiting inside, your answer comes. Simply persistently ask the question. This Spirit won't create a desire for goodness or reveal a truth you're not ready for. You'll receive truth and inspiration as you need it, truth that helps you know God and serve others. Anything beyond this would be pointless and possibly detrimental.

I think this is critical! Insights and guidance we receive are a revelation of God's will for us. It's our challenge and **purpose** to live out this divine will in total surrender, trust, certainty, and enthusiasm. *The point is to change us.* We shouldn't seek guidance to get what we want or avoid problems but to discover how to act to change ourselves to serve others and realize our dreams.

If you try to use God's guidance to get selfish gratification, then you'll never get it. But, if you sincerely wish to dedicate your life to helping others in your family, at work, and in the street, God will flash insight and power to you. God wants you to love for Him, to be His instrument of goodness.

Remember, *all prayers should simply ask for guidance and inspiration on how to act spiritually to solve problems and achieve goals for someone else or ourselves.* Everything else is secondary to this purpose of living because it brings eternal life, happiness, and the inspiration to solve all other problems. God is concerned with our spiritual growth, not whether we have a life of comfort and ease. He wants us to use what we've got through thick and thin to make it all thick.

Through this process much is assumed to be the voice of God. Most of the time we must be careful and recognize these feelings or leadings can be something completely different, usually products of unexpressed thoughts or desires —the unconscious. How often do we dream and think "this is a sign for me"? How many times do we get "a feeling?" Or when was the last time you acted superstiously? Spiritual growth isn't a gaudy display of mystical fireworks and incense, but a gradual enduring legacy of dedicated, selfless living. Therefore, we have to be very careful about identifying a feeling or experience as God's leading. What can we do? How do we know when God has gotten through?

A practical approach will be helpful. Let's assume if a leading or experience brings you or someone closer to God, it's a gift from the Spirit. If an insight leads you or someone to seek the will of God or brings you closer to your ideal self-image, you've been spiritualized. The delightful fact is that everyone is constantly touched in ways they may never realize, the simple, subtle ways of grace.

If we're continuously seeking fantastic experiences, we won't find the stuff of enduring spirituality. To be sure, we'll have moments of spiritual ecstasy and excitement, but the *real* work of your Spirit is the patient energizing of your mind, second by second, day by day. Our attitude must be timeless and dedicated. If we're looking for a show, we aren't looking for spirituality. If you quest for God's way, you're thirsting for life—true spiritual reality.

Fruits of the Spirit-Happiness

In this discussion I've been alluding to spirit gifts. These are God's blessings and what we offer those around us. These gifts and truths have been the center of humanity's quest across time, event after event, through the generations' chain. The source of these gifts is in you! Let's look at them in detail.

Perfect gifts result from a dynamic life with the Spirit. If you know God, then you're increasingly and more effectively living these rewards, showing the fruits. And consequently, once you know God as your Father and others as kin, you're *expected* to bear these fruits, to give something back to God, others, and the universe. The simplest way to bear fruits is to do your utmost through every moment. This is all God expects: He's reasonable and fair. But, if there's no evidence of these fruits in your life, you're spiritually dead. When you do God's will, you will find happiness.

> *To see a man fearless in danger, untainted by lust, happy in adversity, composed in turmoil, and laughing at all those things which are either coveted or feared by others—all men must acknowledge, that this can be nothing else but a beam of divinity animating a human body.*
>
> Seneca

If a person shows the fruits (the spiritual life) this proves she's left the code of evolutionary survival and embraces service. It's proof this person knows God and is filled with the Spirit of God. The person who acts in a way contrary to strict survival instinct has had a religious experience and is on the path to perfection. This person is *happy*.

Spiritual fruits aren't hard to understand; they're simply spiritual traits, ways of living and thinking. The most important is *attitude*. When you have a spiritual life, you're loving and caring, seeking to help anywhere and anytime, tireless and never vengeful. Your life brims with intention to do what's necessary to help. This attitude of love—unconditional love—creates all other love attitudes; your Father-attitude is the foundation for the other spiritual fruits.

This attitude of our Father next affects your *actions*. Envision that all actions can be transformed by the intention of love. In addition, these spiritual movements can have a clarity and purpose designed to achieve perfection, to do the best, and to help others push limits. You'll be *decisive* under the Father's admonishing hand and gain power as you make more and more spiritual decisions. Life will be very productive and stimulating.

As is pointed out here, a new perspective towards people emerges:

> You experience people a lot differently when you try to live the Father's attitude. It's not so much of a competition anymore. It has a lot more to do with cooperation than competition: So, it's no longer my way or your way but let me share my insights with you, let me listen to you and get your insights and we'll see if we can figure out a way and do this together.
>
> The Father's attitude is in some ways looking at somebody as you might look at a ten-year old child of yours or something. How can I help this person get through this hard time they're having? A lot of times, with your expanded viewpoint, you can help a child go through a lot of things that run into problems that you've gone through before; you can help them work through their problems.
>
> It could be a fifty-year old boss: If they're still having a problem that you've run into, you can help them work through that as well. You don't have to be belligerent or unyielding, but more attentive and able to listen to where they're at. Try and understand their viewpoint.

Following on the heels of your attitude and actions will be clear *results* in your growth. You'll transcend the simple struggle and reach strong distinct heights of contact with God. Soon your life will be more productive; you'll be more active and get more results. But, since it's your desire to do the Father's will, you won't try to control the outcome with your expectations, selfish desires, or designs.

Self-control will emerge as you accept the will of the Universal Father. Every non-spiritual desire that goes against knowing God will disappear as your desire to know Him and do His will strengthens. The secret of overcoming problem animal desires is to replace them with spiritual ones. You won't force yourself not to do something but instead gradually lose your growth-impeding desire. Your mind will be spiritualized be recognizing and cultivating spiritual desires and habits, not by trying to merely remove bad habits.

For your life habits you can expect peace, joy, assurance, and happiness. You'll develop a new self-respect giving meaning and purpose but also bringing selflessness and self-forgetfulness. Your life will have unbounded spiritual progress and cooperation with God and every personal character problem that plagues you will evaporate and blow away on the swift breezes.

Let's characterize this new being. Encountering people, your motivation will be love, no matter what they do. Your life will be woven with peace and graciousness and be the picture of faith in action. While you may be passive now, you will be effective, industrious, courageous, and aggressive. Your decisions will be fair, your honesty wise, and your hope will unleash the joy of your associates. You'll be a spiritual being.

Your ideal of behavior and thought will one day be your character, if you choose. And even this will merely begin your eternal progress.

Those who know or contact you will be glad to have been with you because you're a new person who serves and is a true friend. Your life will reflect the loving relationship with your Creator-Father and be a light to many people ignorant of spiritual ways and their Majestic Father. You will be a spiritual pioneer, a truly noble person, a faith child of the Father.

Helping the Spirit, Helping Yourself

The question then becomes, "How do I do it?" To make it, you've got to work and cooperate with the Spirit, allowing God to transform you into a child of light with an eternal destiny. God has some wonderful unknown destiny for *each one* of us. The only way to realize this life is to cooperate with our Spirits and choose to live after death. We need to dedicate ourselves to this supreme effort and priority.

The essence and core of cooperation with the Spirit is in trying to do God's will.

The success of this transformation is dependent on you entirely; you control whether you'll find your spiritual destiny. God awaits your decision and will respect it, whatever the direction. Your Father's Spirit lives in you, works in you, and hopes for your cooperation but will only do that which you've assented to and asked for. Never will this Spirit go against your will, even though you may choose to go against the Father's will. Creating your eternal soul with God's Spirit requires your cooperation. Your Spirit can't make a change in you unless you cooperate!

The only way to become more than you are is to give all you are to do God's will.

The next three ingredients of this uplifting process are likewise wholly dependent on you. God gives the hunger for truth, the ability to act without seeing proof—Faith, and the environment in which to decide. If you sincerely seek the truth and act without proof, you'll have an eternal destiny. Your Father gives the raw materials of spiritual desire and inspiration. All that's needed is intelligent cooperation, the consecration of your will to His will. Nothing in your spiritual experience is determined or actualized without your will.

Of course, total dedication to doing God's will is challenging and demanding. Often we find we're more strongly influenced by survival instincts and resultant behaviors (our minds filled with disturbing thoughts) than by God. These images born of fear and laziness block God's whisper. We do have two influences—God and nature. However, resistance only occurs when we choose nature and our own selfishness above God and His will.

This is a common problem:

> Probably the biggest thing is just not listening, not taking the time to listen. I think meditation is really valuable. A daily habit of meditation really allows you to stop and get input from the Spirit.
>
> A lot of times it seems like you don't have time or you're too busy to stop and take that time. In reality, that's the best thing you can do, to stop and take that time because it will help you coordinate all the other stuff, stuff that you're busy going about doing. If you just do it without taking time to relate it, to organize it, it's real inefficient; you won't get much done. If you organize it, if you put it in relationship with God, it'll be a lot more effective, have a lot more power.
>
> I guess the main way of blocking the Spirit is not taking time to listen.

What's gained from resisting God, trying to throw away the greatest treasure, eternal life? We're *designed* to know God, but not forced into it. Why do we put off changes we know would bring us happiness and success? Why must we move so slowly and risk spiritual progress for momentary personal gratification and pleasure-seeking selfishness? Do these choices make sense?

Whatever your choice, God is patient and knows what you really want; He knows your heart. So, don't worry. Our Father sees our intentions even through the mist of our confusion and stubbornness. The Father knows whether you want to be stubborn or just haven't figured out how to change or are purposefully against Him. God is fair.

Following the root of our will—our decisions—is the way we carry them out. The opposite of the survival tendencies of sloth and fear are *courage* and *industry*. When we embrace truth and act without seeing proof of spiritual outcomes or benefit, we must ask for courage and industry. When these are supplied, God's will is done to the best of our ability; we grow tremendously.

In addition, after we've faced a problem or chosen a goal, it's time to make plans. When we make these decisions of living, we should always ask God what He thinks about our reasoning or plan of action. When we do this, we'll receive the guidance and help we need, not before! Do the homework first.

Now that we understand the essentials, it's time to look at cooperation techniques to help our personal Spirit guides.

When you experience God's leading, *follow it*. Let's say you have an important decision to make; you have to decide what to say to a friend for he's insulted you many times before. You've planned to get together to ski and have for several days been formulating different things to say to your friend. Sit down and ask God what's best. Don't stop listening until you're sure of an answer. Life is filled with these and other endless opportunities to seek God's advice.

Secondly, dedicate every day to help God with His plan; *love God and strive to be like Him*. We must understand that God has a place in His plan only we can fill. How can we not love God when we experience His love, when He provides abundantly and is so kind and gentle? Determine to do something for God for your life's duration; do His will. Make the imitation of God your standard.

Next, regard your sisters and brothers with *love* and *service*. Think about the people in your life, and when they need help, give it in a way they'll appreciate. Do it unconditionally. Maybe a neighbor needs help shoveling the sidewalk; maybe your spouse needs someone to talk to; maybe your child wants to spend more time with you. Move to understand the people around you to really love and serve them.

And finally, realize you have something unique to give that God needs; *understand you have a responsibility to help God.* Your experiences become a part of God's experience. You add something new and dynamic to the universe when you strive to live fully and are living the potentials of God's infinite nature. Just think! You have the chance to express life originally, uniquely. You can be an artist.

By weaving these spiritual understandings and habits, you'll find a growth unimagined, not by mysterious forces or fantastic displays, but by steady, patient devoted living for God and humankind. One phrase says it: You are doing the Father's will.

As said here, we can make a contribution:

> It's an amazing thought. I go outside and look at the sky at night. When you look at the stars and the planets, and you see everything evolving, it makes you feel so small and humble: You know that God is the creator of all this. I realize that in some important way my puny little life is a critical piece of all this. The experiences that I live that I turn around and give to God, if I don't live them to the fullest spiritually, if I don't wholeheartedly offer them to God, the evolution of this whole universe is gonna be just a little bit different, there'll be a little piece of it missing if I don't give it to it. It's an amazing thought.

> It's exciting. I keep talking about the eternal adventure. There's just nothing more thrilling than being a part of this.

It boils down to this: We must meet the needs of body, mind, and Spirit to grow. Judiciously help your body by exercising, eating well, and attending to medical conditions. Nourish your mind by learning what will help you live spiritually and meet basic needs. Live in your civilization to succeed at work and thrive with your family and friends.

Spend time with God and your Spirit by praying, worshiping, and meditating; make time for spiritual food. In all these areas, develop ideal and beneficial habits that provide the highest sustenance. Allow your entire being to be unified in a three-fold coordination for doing the will of God.

> *For one who is disciplined in eating and recreation, who engages himself in actions in a disciplined manner, who properly regulates his sleep and wakefulness . . . When one's properly controlled mind becomes steadfast within the Self alone and when one becomes free . . . he finds that supreme bliss . . . he does not swerve from reality.*
>
> *Bhagavad Gītā*

It's your will, once and for all, that determines everything because its intensity and direction brings you to God or drives you away. Make the decision to do all for God. When you make a decision with God, your will strengthens and is allowed greater expression because you're acting in concert with Him. This doing of the will of God is not a lessening of your will but an amplification through chosen cooperation with God.

If you imitate God, you become more like Him. Since God is the source of will and life, you become more aware, more self-conscious, more alive. You're no longer an unconscious reflection of the environment, but a conscious reflection of God's nature and an actor in the environment. The definition of self-consciousness is: self-determination and inner motivation, spiritual independence from the environment.

You're only self-conscious (self-determined) when you make a decision to act on inner leadings, moral leadings. To merely react to the outer world is to fall asleep and forget you're alive, becoming a mere instrument of the world; you've given up self-control and self-determination, pieces of self-consciousness! Each time you choose to avoid spiritual decisions, you go unconscious a bit more; you die a bit more. Continued unhappiness is the warning sign of spiritual disease and eventual eternal death. However, the environment does not determine the way we live if we base our lives on spiritual experience, God's leading.

To ignore inner leadings is to sleep through life, to surrender to the environment. The fully living person bases life on the inner world practically applied to the outer. When you choose to do God's will, you and the Spirit are **one** for that decision and set of actions and are *living*. Learn to know this and taste it.

When you've done these things, the Spirit can do more for you; then can you choose faith, seeking truth, courage, and industry; then can you be a spiritual child of God.

Your Spirit is from God who loves with a perfect sublime divine motivation. Every moment this friend is trying to bring you up into the heights of glory and destiny. Will you choose to help your champion? Will you awake to the delightful challenge of seeking God and serving others? It's your choice. Allow the Spirit to touch you. Place your life in God's hands.

Dedicate your every energy and intention to cooperation with God's Spirit. Nothing else is more important.

May you do the will of our Father.

May you Grow!

Spiritual Truths

We need help to overcome fear and sloth!

Our Father has given each of us
a perfect Spirit teacher and friend.

Our teachers' purpose is to help us
do our Father's will to become eternal.

Our Spirit Teachers work with our minds.

To cooperate with our teachers, we must do
our Father's will and accept the truth.

We are destined to be with our friends
forever in eternal growth.

G r o w t h

Becoming Eternal
Chapter 8

O

Imagine you've been entrusted with a delicate medicinal plant. There are two reasons why your trust is so crucial. First, this plant alleviates many forms of heart disease, and secondly, it has been almost annihilated by a combination of land development and farm chemicals. The possible gains are so great that this plant must be safeguarded and fostered. It's assured you'll do everything in your power and take any risk to preserve this irreplaceable form of life.

I believe most of us would be honored with this task and be true to our trusts. The fact is, all of us have been given trusts of much greater significance and consequence, namely, the care and fostering of our spiritual selves—our souls. As careful and patient as we would be with a plant or other living creature, so must we exercise utmost intent and action in our spiritual lives. We must provide for our needs and those of others.

Characterizing Growth

Growth is everything. Growth indicates our spiritual experience and simultaneously gives a prelude to future possibilities and destinies. Becoming more and more like our Father is our ultimate gift to Him.

God expects us to go the distance. The Father gives life and commands us to become perfect in our own way, to touch the divine light and reach up through the stars to a boundless universe panorama. In fact, it's our *duty* to take each day as an occasion to transcend imperfect living to reach for the light. Everything we do should lead toward perfection. If you've begun the growth process (taken your Spirit's leadings to heart) no limit can be placed on the marvelous destiny that awaits you here and in the afterlife. The bliss of growth can be yours.

> Could any task be more important
>   than my work?
> Any challenge more worthy
>   than the spiritual journey?
> Any promise more valuable
>   than eternal life?
>
>   Merritt Horn

Our spiritual lives are like other forms of life. If something isn't growing, it has died. Once a seed's been planted it begins to grow to maturity or succumbs to malnutrition, disease, etc. It's unavoidable that we have spiritual leadings and possible destinies and are filled with the Spirit of God. When you realize you're a child of God and all people are sisters and brothers, **you must begin to make choices** which transform you into a spiritual being. If you cease to make any spiritual choices, you've destroyed yourself and discarded the greatest treasure— life eternal.

But, when you choose to become like God, you begin the hopeful path of doing the impossible. You leave personal weaknesses that gave you so much unhappiness by transforming them into the fruits of the Spirit. When you decide to do the Father's will, you'll get all the time you need to grow. If you're sincere in this growth process, you have eternity to become like God (God is extremely patient.)!

And since our Father has given you a personal Spirit friend, guide, and transformer, there's no limit to your growth. God is endless and infinite, and so must be our growth, for it is, in the first and final sense, the quest for God. We'll be intrigued with growth for eternity!

These people have considered the implications:

> We're finite beings and we tend to think of things in starts, middles, and *ends*. So, we want to make sure by the time the end comes around that we've *got* it, that we're perfect, that we made it, made the grade, all these things. When you come to realize there is a continuum, then you can really be present in the present moment. You don't have to accomplish all the goals of existence today; you accomplish today's goals; you accomplish tomorrow's goals tomorrow. The continuum is a very comforting thought.

> It's both comforting and disturbing at the same time to know I'll always be growing. Because of my finiteness, there's a desire to want to get things finalized, cleaned up, done, accomplished so we can kick back, have freedom from assignment. We'd like to get to that point, O.K. When we think about the fact that we can always, always get better, it's kind of . . . on one level there'll always be more to do.

> That brings up a really interesting thing 'cause most of us really have that thought that we want to get done with it, so to speak, so that we can sit on the porch, kick our feet up, and watch the world go by. It's just really not gonna go that way. That's a utopian concept . . . there'll always be things to be done; there'll always be things to be gained from doing those things.

> The comforting side of that thought is that as a result of that we can just go at a pace that is human and stay in touch with ourselves at the present moment and continue to enjoy the process. A friend of mine one time told me when I was involved in some quandary or dilemma, "Well if you can't enjoy the process I have no

respect for you at all." And it really was a wake up call
for me to hear that because it made me come to realize
that it's the method as much as it is the goal that we
gain by. The fact that the continuum just continues, lets
us just do what we do.

Many people believe growth is only for one's development. But, if you give expression and are sensitive to service
urges you'll see these transformations benefit others as much
as yourself. The soul's alchemy is a reciprocal process where
everyone grows by helping others. We must realize the
universe isn't at our command and we should take the
humble attitude of an innocent child willing to help a friend.

In the matrix of life, everyone is a thread, part of the
bright tapestry of spiritual living and discovery. Each of us
exists only in relation to the masterpiece God weaves; we
don't have life in and of ourselves. If the masterpiece begins
to grow and unfold, each thread benefits and experiences
increased capacity and progress. If those around us are slow
in progressing, we must adjust our lives accordingly. Everyone is rewarded when we pursue the spiritual path: Everyone
benefits by the godly actions of one person and that person
benefits by the godly actions of everyone else.

The multitude of people throughout the universe are
necessary for God's plan. God needs us! He generously gives
us life and a spiritual destiny so we may do His will in a step
by step contribution to His plan. Our every spiritual experience is channeled to God through the divine Spirits living in
us and helps God to His goal. We're partners with God.

The funny thing about growth is that we don't know it's
happening: We only know it's *happened*. Growth is completely unconscious. By taking a backward glance we're able
to see we've grown, but none of us *feels* it happening. When
we grow, the Spirit creates a part of us we've never known
—continual soul growth—which we only see later when we
look at the Spirit's work and see change. When acting

spiritually we can't observe our souls because our minds are involved in decision making; our attention can only be in one place. This is our fascinating continual rebirth.

As was said earlier, there's nothing that can stop you if you want to grow. You can make spiritual decisions any- where and anytime and be comforted that your Spirit is continually giving you what you need to grow. If you want to, no obstacle can keep you from doing God's will. *Our decisions can become absolutely independent of our environ- ment, possessions, or home, when we live spiritually.*

Growth is our purpose and deepens life, for life is the spiritual. If you experience real life as contrasted to animal life, you're feeling the spiritual, the superhuman, your ability to know God and do His will. If we're not doing God's will, we're not truly human. When we strive to fulfill our growth commission, we're saturated with life, all improves, and we enter and become part of an undreamed-of world.

When we think certain changes are impossible it's because we see things in an animal way. But, if you have the Spirit's vision—your soul—you'll see what's really possible with God's help. You can live the life of your dreams beyond your ideals!

When people live such a life, they're inspiring. They become cosmic cheerleaders for the supernal game of eternity —growth, the matchless nobility of leaving an animal, limited life behind. Everybody is suddenly a powerful craftsman working on the same project of celestial growth. We're reaching for the same goal, living for the Father's will, and helping each other with inspiration and understanding service. Progress, progress is the way of creation. And, you're part of it. Join in! You were meant for progress. Every child of God starts with an *equal* chance for spiritual progress and gets what he or she needs to achieve this spiritual progress.

If you're sincere in your quest, nothing you do or say gets in the way. God knows what you really desire to do and become; He knows your intentions. Focusing your will to do the Father's will assures you'll realize the full spiritual life you're capable of—an eternity of growth. We're from different backgrounds and environments, but everyone is equal before God and has an equal chance to become like Him.

To be a little uncertain of the future only shows you're human like the rest of us. There's nothing wrong with this. In fact, uncertainty is the true spice of life, a curtain drawn on fascinating events just ahead, the enticement that makes life interesting and unpredictable.

Let's listen in:

> Uncertainty is that little stimulating factor that keeps us evolutionary creatures from acting just like water: Water settles into the lowest possible point, sits and stagnates unless something comes and moves it around. That uncertainty is that agitation we seem to need to keep moving, to keep rolling along. It's something that brings about the unfolding, the discovery process, and the evolutionary process. If everything was certain and all predetermined, I'd feel more like a puppet in a play than actor in a play.
>
> That uncertainty, while it can rattle your cage from time to time, also provides the opportunity. Chaos is as much an opportunity as it is anything else . . . What you have is a constant series of problem-solving predicaments that comes to you. A lot of times they're slow to solve and hard to make work. I've always said that character's what you get when you can't get nothin' else. You're staring at a hundred miles of problems and every solution to work with: What you come up with is character.
>
> . . . There's endless numbers of problems to solve. Problem-solving is what makes people successful in life anyway. Life is a series of problems that need to be solved. People who are enjoying life are the people that get good *at problem-solving*.

If we knew the future, what would our lives be like? I suppose it would be like seeing the same movie over again, no suspense, thrill, or enjoyment, just a dull programmed artificial animation. No! We don't want to know the future but want to jump out and risk everything for doing the Father's will, for serving humankind. Only by being willing to *risk everything* can we overcome our animal selves. There's no real risk without uncertainty . . .

. . . When you grow, it's always nice to look back on past endeavors and accomplishments, but, sometimes we tend to judge ourselves against these! Don't be concerned with your current level of achievement but instead be concerned with your attitude and effort: You have eternity to grow. The most important revelation is that you are growing, moving forward. Growth is a steady, slow, evolutionary process. Be like a seed and work patiently each moment, each day.

The Nature of Life

Understanding life can be complicated because we try to think about everything at once. Cultivating a spiritual self amidst the intricacies of our complex time is most perplexing. To do this, let's first examine life.

Everyone must do certain things: Everybody sleeps, eats, finds a place to live and a way to support themselves. You wake up, begin your day, think about what you need to do, and then go about doing it or not. You go out into the world and begin your work, encounter problems, and then try to solve or avoid them. Every decision you make has a result you experience.

Suppose you need milk. If you don't act on this need, you won't get the milk or its benefits. Everything revolves around filling needs in a way that benefits our lives or taking the consequences of ignoring these requirements. Everybody meets his or her needs to varying degrees and, in turn, experiences different rewards and detriments.

But what is a need? A need is something we must have to nourish our *bodies, minds, or souls*: We need food, shelter, clothing, protection, medical treatment; we must understand how to live a good life, how to get what we need, communicate with others and share their company, and use our minds to solve problems; we need to live with God and bring His inspiration and guidance into the way we live. Every human being has these three sets of needs which must be satisfied for a whole, balanced life, needs of body, mind, and spirit.

Simultaneous with filling our needs, we fill the needs of others, a complete symbiosis. This happens increasingly as we meet our spiritual needs (the needs governing the whole process) because the spiritual technique benefits everyone. All our needs should be enlisted to provide spiritual growth in ourselves and others. *In fact, the primary technique is to help others grow.* This is true spirituality.

Every time we try to satisfy a need, we inevitably make a decision to act or not. Every intention brings certain repercussions helping us meet our needs or not. The more decisions you make to meet your needs, the more those needs will be met and the more you'll grow, while if you act in ways that don't meet your needs, you'll experience the consequences—unhappiness, separation from God.

Happiness is the result of an active life of rigor and courage. If you're not making decisions or putting them off, don't expect an improvement. But, if you're willing to be forthright and brave, be assured you'll feel better.

Growth is happiness. By utilizing our bodies and minds to do God's will, we help His Spirit create our souls. If you're truly happy, you've been living with God and challenging yourself to do His will at all costs. If you're not happy, you're not doing God's will; you're not growing.

To understand growth, let's look at the ingredients which make us human.

The miracle of life comes when combining the aspects of our being. God gives us a will to direct our tools and this *will* is the secret and determining factor of our spiritual experience. You can determine whether you achieve destiny as a child of God; you decide what to do with what you've been given.

Your mind is a window to the world and the levers you move to live in it. The mind knows the outside world through images and other sensory input along with accompanying feelings. It also provides desires, urges, and propensities towards survival and acting effectively in that world. Your mind is the channel of communication allowing you to know other people and think about them. Here you plan, figure out, and see your choices.

God also gives us a body, our tool for living. It's the body that acts out what the will has decided and brings to the mind the experience of the environment. And lastly, in the midst of your being is your personal Spirit, your transformer to the divine.

Because we have will, we're compelled to make decisions: The decision-making process is the gift of God. It doesn't matter what you do; you're always making decisions; whatever problem has crept into your life, it will always and unfailing require you to make some decision.

Here's a view on decisions:

> Decisions are the actual steps of growth. You can be wishy-washy about a lot of things and not really decide to do something where you kind of go around in circles. Decisions are really taking an actual step in the direction.
>
> The difference between a dream or a vision of what could be . . . there's two ways to approach it: You could just sit there and have that vision, that dream, and not do anything towards it, you'll never achieve it, or you can start taking steps along the way, making little decisions. "If I want this to happen, then the next step

is to do this." When you get to that step, then you'll be able to say, "Well now I'm here. Now the next step to get that dream is to do this." It's like a cascade effect. The next result is directly dependent on what just happened. It builds.

Here we are. Let's be frank. The place we live, earth, is quite a mess and each of us its product and a little like it, imperfect and confused. But, what an adventure we have set before us! People have the potential of growing spiritually, becoming true, beautiful, and good in life's ways, and can use their will to create or destroy their gifts. We must live in the world; there's no avoiding the responsibilities of life.

The future of mankind lies waiting for those who will come to understand their lives and take up their responsibilities to all living things.

Vine Victor Deloria, Jr.

Growth is an exclamation point in the life story. We should want to be courageous, intelligent, tactful, industrious, understanding, loyal, unselfish, idealistic, and effective. It's natural that our animal instincts rebel against this change (They don't like hard work.). Everyone shares this experience of animal resistance and inertia.

Let's remember that our world and ourselves must be this way to bring out spiritual qualities: We need a challenge if we are to grow and be the real spiritual beings of God. There's a reason for our process of growth. God knows what He's doing and clearly created us and our world with these propensities in order to bring us happiness. Without the struggle of life, no one would find happiness or satisfaction.

Please understand, God gives you everything indispensable for growth. You have freewill, a body, a mind, and an unfailing perfect Spirit teacher. Look around at the world of risk and achievement. The merciful Father plants the fire of growth, the urge to become better and be true to the nature of God. Can we have imagined a more glorious destiny and enviable process?

The key to this entire process is **you**. If you cooperate with God, then you'll live forever, becoming more and more like God, growing for eternity, and helping others to do the same. The decision will always be yours at every crossroad and set of alternatives.

The Growth Process Essentials

At this moment we're poised at the very beginning of our careers as children of the Father. It's crucial we concentrate on growth methods as well as supplying the nourishment so essential to this growth.

Once and for all, let's be clear on why we're here. *Our purpose is to become like God in the way we live.* Everything else must be secondary to living the ways of truth, beauty, and goodness. At the same time we recognize this as our supreme goal, we must realize that other goals are transitory scaffolding to building this immortal future.

The standard for our conduct must be God; we should gleefully strive to be as God in our characters. This means every priority impeding us from doing the Father's will must be avoided or eliminated while the sum of our energies and actions—our *loyalty*—are dedicated to God and His plan. How could anything be more important or necessary in life?

Sooner or later all universe personalities begin to realize that the final quest of eternity is the endless exploration of infinity, the never-ending voyage of discovery into the absoluteness of the First Source and Center. Sooner or later we all become aware that all creature growth is proportional to Father identification. We arrive at the understanding that living the will of God

*is the eternal passport to the endless possibility of
infinity itself. Mortals will sometime realize that success
in the quest of the Infinite is directly proportional to the
achievement of Fatherlikeness . . .*

The Urantia Book

This doing of the Father's will means we bring every
important decision to Him to gain His advice and inspiration,
to follow truth and light and be unafraid of family, friends,
and society, and to make any sacrifice to follow this advice.
Surrendering with utmost resolve and candor, we can
embrace real life, a way of living merging with the Spirit.

In the moments you touch God, you've elected to embark
on a decision with God, to amplify and extend the power and
meaning of your intent up to eternal reaches. Your decisions
gain a real *value* and significance to the degree they're in
accordance with the Father's will. We should be completely
absorbed in the graceful, endearing living of the Father's will.
We should do what God wants us to and do everything the
way He intends. We should become brilliant lighthouses of
direction and hope.

This quotation illustrates the experience of God's will:

It feels right. It feels warm; it feels like on a correct
path. I feel like He's looking down and saying, "Right on!
You've got it now." I just feel like I'm enveloped by His
righteousness, His power, His love. I wanna do it more.

When I'm doing service projects and helping other
people . . . I think anything that you do that is selfless,
it can be feeding the hungry, it can be being a mother.
That's the biggest example right now in my life because
you can't be selfish: That baby cries, you have to go to
it; you have to do for the baby before you.

I feel like this is one of His sons or daughters and
He sent it to me to take care of. Right now that's my
biggest example of doing the Father's will. And I feel like
it's a lifetime commitment. I'm thrilled to do it.

The result of doing the Father's will is an unlimited future of endless glory, while its converse is death. If we don't choose the Father's will, we slowly determine to destroy ourselves. Just as doing God's will reinforces and gives life, the blatant disregard of and rebellion to God closes our minds and souls to spirit gifts—life.

Ultimately, we're the architects of our death if we stubbornly refuse to help others. The self lives because it not only preserves itself, but because it delights in loving friendship and brotherhood. It dies when it denies God's presence and the need to serve others. In choosing God's will, we simply say we enjoy life.

This brings us right back to decisions because they constantly influence our minds and souls. Every decision is based on one of two ways of reacting: Either you act on purely self-preservation instincts or you act to help others; you choose the animal way or the spiritual. No one can elude the inexorable fact that we'll act in a spiritual or a material way. As time goes on, hopefully we'll listen to our Spirits and choose the spiritual solution to the material problem.

If you want to grow, seek spiritual things; do the Father's will. Live for the benefit of others.

These decisions are born of a process that's constant and ever-present when you're conscious. At this moment your mind is filled with *urges, needs, conflicts, problems, and visions*, each requiring you to do something or nothing. Think about them and realize your reaction to them is a choice.

The decision you make will be a *plan*, an envisioned action to satisfy the urge, need, conflict, problem, or vision. It may be that you're going to drive to the store for popcorn, or you decide to apologize to a neighbor for a loud party. Whatever it is, you feel compelled to do something about it, that is, carry out a plan.

Finally, you make the actual decision after thinking about your plan. When you forcefully do something, you've made a *decision*, not before then. After you make the decision, you experience the result of your actions, body, mind, or soul change, and new urges, needs, conflicts, problems, and visions emerge to begin the growth cycle again requiring more decisions, but now at the next higher level.

Step by step it's your will that determines which urges to follow, needs to fill, conflicts to address, visions to achieve, and how you'll do it. You'll also be doing this at every step along the way, from problem to plan to decision to result. All is determined by your will.

The sure path to growth is letting God into every step of growth. When you get an urge, need, problem, conflict, or vision, ask God for help and inspiration. When you think you have a good plan, listen to God's advice and organize your energies for action while asking God for strength and courage to make the decision. And when you experience the fruits or disappointments of your actions or life's uncertainties, let God love and caress you with a fatherly hand. Share everything with God.

You'll find the splendid results of growth will be an increased capacity to grow and be happy, an enlarging relationship with God, a greater experience of God, and a way of life more in tune with God.

Each of us has the potential to grow by the Creator's grace. Our loving Father provides all we'll need along the intriguing journey of existence. There's no joy that's impossible and no wonder that can't be seen. We've been blessed with life, a life of growth. It's up to us.

Spiritual Truths

We exist to Grow.

When we grow we become like our Father
in the way we live.

Our Father expects us to grow.

Our growth is unlimited and endless.

Growth is for everyone's benefit.

We must have discipline to grow.

Growing

Getting Down to Business
Chapter 9

O

In a sense, acceptance is the easy part of spiritual life. Believing in God and your fellows is more an act of heart than of mind, but, to mature as a full-grown spiritual being, you must be willing to *live* your beliefs, to do what's necessary.

Often we've been lulled to take the simple path, the relaxed path. While there will always be escapes to avoid self-examination and hard work, necessary choices are unavoidable; it's "pay me now or pay me later." If you want to live forever in a universe of adventure, you've got to act adventurously and timelessly. It's time to put up or shut up; you must get down to business.

How to Grow

Priorities, priorities, and more priorities determine growth. If you dedicate, focus, risk, and give all of yourself to live spiritually, you'll grow. In fact, **to grow, you must give everything you are and have,** willing to risk it all for God's will, for your friends.

> *When man consecrates his will to the doing of the*
> *Father's will, when man gives God all that he has, then*
> *does God make that man more than he is.*
>
> *The Urantia Book*

What matters to you? What do you think about? What activities occupy your work day and leisure hours? Where do you want to be in five years, or twenty years? What do you desire? What do you wish to achieve? What are you willing to sacrifice for? Be honest and take a moment . . .

. . . If you feel God's presence and know all people are your brothers and sisters, what do you desire? Please realize *this determines your growth*, thoughts, and actions. If you want to grow, you must seek the spiritual way of life and drink spiritual realities. By doing this first you'll be on the certain path to an endless future of service and concrete happiness, but without this decision you won't progress. You must make this first and constant determination to put your totality into celestial conduct. Have spiritual goals.

Our next step is to keep in mind that everything in life is merely transitory to helping people know God and to progress. This is the true test of value. The homes we live in meet a need; the music we dance to supplies a release; the salaries we reach for give us sustenance. But all these are means to help get us to our destination—God. This is the pure light to view life in. Let your vision reveal the passing nature of these things and embrace real value—loving relationships.

Devote yourself to being the best according to your highest values, principles, and ideals. Make these the lures to beckon you to well-defined mountain tops of refreshing and invigorating spiritual ecstasy and exertion. Learn to glean beautiful gems that make life better and help you know God and serve others, to stand firm, steadfast, and unwavering on

what you know is right! Don't be afraid, but rather be willing
to risk everything for your spiritual values and God's will.

When there's a choice, choose sacrifice instead of
pleasure. Learn to find real meanings and substitute these for
the endless pursuit of physical stimulation, power, and
material goals that so often engulf us. When you've learned
to choose spiritual actions over raw desires, you've learned to
walk with God in grace and unity.

This person speaks of the difficult choices:

> When we were living in New York, we had gone to
> a lecture . . . it was kind of like a short notice. We found
> out that there was a seminar offered that weekend that
> just sounded really powerful: It was about relationships
> in the broadest sense, not just with each other but
> everybody in your life all the way up to and including
> your relationship with God.
>
> It was kind of awkward because we were supposed
> to go skiing in Vermont with some people that we're real
> close to. We were really looking forward to the ski
> weekend. But then we found out like the Wednesday
> before that there was that seminar offered that week-
> end. I think we felt compelled to go to this thing. Even
> though it certainly wouldn't be as much fun sitting in a
> hotel room doing a seminar as being at skiing, we just
> sensed that it was something that was real important to
> us to do. We both agreed on that. We knew that we
> wanted to do that even though it meant forgoing the
> skiing and disappointing our friends.
>
> We knew it was the right thing to do. We did it and
> it kind of inspired us and really helped to set us on a
> path. It ended up definitely being the right thing to do
> even though it meant forgoing a fun weekend.

As in the anecdote, we must act. When you have an urge
to help another, do it *intensely*. When you have a spiritual
leading, vision, or insight, do your utmost to unfurl your
spirit-mind. Take every survival instinct, every selfish desire,
and convert it, renew it, elevate it, transform it to the spirit

level of unselfish service. Replace selfishness with service, fear with courage, inaction with industry, ego ugliness with spiritual beauty, evil with good, frustration with patience, hate with love, and darkness with illumination. Take your will and determine to do the Father's will.

When you've thought about what you need to do and sought God's will, and you're certain it's right, do it! This always brings you closer to God.

Even if you make a mistake and haven't understood God, the pure sincere effort to do His will assures you've grown and will be that much closer the next time you try. Just as we expect our children to have gradual slow maturation and understanding, and recognize that they're going to misunderstand us once in a while, our Universal Father touchingly cheers all our awkward efforts as well as our triumphs. It's obvious we'll goof, but it's also obvious we'll never learn if we're rigid or lazy and don't try to do the Father's will.

Simply put, when you encounter problems to solve, needs to meet, and conflicts to resolve, meet with God and talk; spend time with God. Tell the Father what's on your mind and **listen** to what He says or the way He leads you. Go to God and touch Him, trust, embrace, and act with faith, instead of sitting by, waiting to see the future.

I think the most important aspect of this adventure is faith. You have to be able to act without seeing where your decisions are leading and must be able to step off and risk, to trust our wise Father. You should enthusiastically act without seeing why or how your actions will lead to spiritual growth. Your task is to do the right thing, the unseen thing, living the ways of the spiritual world. Without using the leadings of God, the feelings of security and trust, you won't progress. God already lets you know everything is going to be fine: This is *faith*. Act in accordance with your trust in God.

This growth process takes a tremendous effort of superhuman resolve. You're engaged in transforming yourself into a completely new person, a spiritual artist, and as designer of your new self, must take the long and demanding road with a dedication to give all to growth. It's not until we give all we are that a problem is solved or a new quality emerges. This is profound.

Think about the training so many of us have gone through. Well, we're engaged in the training of the Spirit, of eternal life, the most important training of all. Think of its significance and usefulness. Our rate of growth is determined by the amount of effort we bear on spiritual movement. Put everything you've got into this process. Concentrate the total powers of your being on doing the Father's will and trust things will work out for the benefit of your spiritual development. Focus your will on life in a spiritual way; pour yourself out in a ministry to your fellows as the hand of God.

Finding every opportunity to grow is the secret of an active life. Act, act, and act some more on your leadings. By acting constantly we exercise that new spiritual part—the soul—and transform more of our old selves. Action is the ultimate catalyst where your Spirit makes you a new person; nevertheless, without your consecrated actions, the Spirit is utterly powerless. You must act!

> A tree that it takes both arms to encircle grew from a tiny rootlet. A many storied pagoda is built by placing one brick upon another brick. A journey of three thousand miles is begun by a single step.
>
> Lao Tzu

And who said it would be easy, quick, and made to order? When you chose to board the spiritual vehicle, you had to know it would take a long time, but a delightful time. In a way, the journey is where we find our greatest treasures, not simply by reaching a goal, because most of the time we're doing just that, traveling and biding our time. So, be persistent and patient. Know you must try, again, and again, forever. After all, who achieves great things without persistence?

Also, we must be courageous to overcome the natural fear and laziness inherited from our evolutionary past. Learn to act with a fearless resolve and focus your strength on achieving your goal and remember that from this dedicated action all spiritual growth comes and that these repeated noble patterns crystalize into life-giving habits. When we act with courage and industry with God, all things are possible.

If you're sincere, hunger for truth, and act with faith, you'll grow. Pledge yourself only to these things, fill your life with them, and you'll be an eternal child of God and know His joy. Let all others enjoy your service.

Nourishing Your Growth

Imagine that you go to a tree nursery and select the most promising tree, a young aspen. Carefully you read the planting and watering instructions and find a good place to plant with the proper hole depth and position. Through the years you'll do everything you can to ensure this tree's success and endurance.

Would you let the $150 investment of that tree be neglected to the point of death? Would you waste and squander the gifts of eternal life and soul growth which God places in your hands? We have to avoid complacency! Always must we challenge ourselves on the road of spiritual discovery and nourish our growth in spite of the inertia of the world around.

Needs cannot be ignored without experiencing undue stress and unhappiness. The real key is to balance the needs of the self with the needs of the others surrounding you. Let's face it, it's tricky to decide when to forgo a pleasure or to extend yourself to help someone. At what point are we giving or taking too much? When does the self become truly selfish or completely self-effacing to the point of neglect? It is critical that we spend time in spiritual nourishment so that we will have the objective point of view from God on these matters in addition to self-examination. We will have the right amount of self-respect, not too much or too little. We will know how to take care of our goals, dreams, and desires as well as those of others. And also remembering that many times the most effective service one can give is to allow someone to serve *you*.

The first factor in spiritual growth is the nourishing of the person. Nothing else will follow without it. Expecting yourself to grow without spiritual food is like expecting a farmer to grow crops without water, air, and sun. This is our first duty of spiritual growth, attending to our needs, so let's examine it.

While I've emphasized the soul needs, we shouldn't neglect our minds and bodies, for every time we use them, we use energy; when you have to think or make decisions based on God's will, you use real energy. *All* these energies must be replenished! The interesting consequence is that if we neglect any of these areas, it affects the other two, and thus the whole process. You surely can grow if all things aren't balanced, but the best way to grow is by meeting the needs of the body, mind, and soul through proper care, education and socialization, and prayer and worship.

This woman discusses one method:

> Pray. Last night I was laying in bed and I usually meditate at night because I'm too sleepy in the morning to concentrate. So I always meditate the last thing before I go to bed (or fall asleep). And I remember making this instruction to my brain: What I wanted to do was to connect with the Infinite; I wanted to pull myself out of my day to day situation and see things in a wider scale. So I utilize whatever source of symbols that are working with my mind at that time.

I remember when the babies were really small. I used to have to feed them at all hours of the night. We would sometimes just be sitting there in pitch black. Because I was just laying there for hours and hours with this bottle, for *hours* with both of them, I would shut my eyes and try to meditate and pray while I was doing this stuff 'cause I couldn't fall asleep . . .

. . . That's what I do to renew my spiritual energy, to step back or step away and see things from a larger perspective which for *me* means seeing things more physically in a large universe scale. Being able to renew my spiritual energy because I've stepped away from things.

The same thing happens to me when I'll be talking to someone and a truth . . . you know how you'll experience a truth; the truth will really hit home for you. And you are just sort of connected for that moment very consciously, very strongly, with God. At those times, I again pull out of my perspective. That really seems to be it because it seems like I have all the energy I need. It's just that I don't know it because I become so small-minded that I can't see my way out of these self-imposed limitations.

But, in fact, all these things that seem so important aren't really at all. I've got all the time in the world. And so, that makes me relax. When I relax I'm not so defensive. When I'm not so defensive I seem to be able to take in more spiritual energy.

The parts work together to perform the function of spiritual living. When we use our will, we use our bodies or our minds. By making sure you're healthy, thinking clearly, and spending time with God, you give tremendous power to your will: You can make great spiritual decisions. We're designed this way. All areas depend on each other.

Just as this balanced living is beneficial, putting too much emphasis on any area is bad. Suppose you thought you'd spend most of your time with God, praying all the time, going off alone. How in the world would you be able to relate with people since you'd be out of touch, a virtual social misfit? And, what if you spent all your time partying and playing? What of the nourishment your soul requires? Every part must have its needs met in a sane and healthy way. Develop clean and spiritual habits of mind and body. Learn a balanced life and your Spirit will have the best chance to work with you.

The common element in meeting these manifold needs is time. You must set aside the appropriate time for each of your needs. If you know you should take time out to speak to God, turn off the T.V., forego the movie, or put down the book and ponder what's important and make a decision based on intelligent reflection. Exercise regularly and make your body an effective friend in living a fruitful, healthy life. Simplify your life to do fewer things to spend more time on basics.

When we don't put in the time we're reduced to unconscious creatures of strict survival reactions. The animal takes over completely and says the cruel word, does the wrong thing, or worse, forgets about growth. The more conscious you are of your actions, the more real you become, the more you're like the Father. Whatever the other activity (God knows we have a perplexing infinity of them.), *forget it until your simple needs are filled.* Nothing else is more important to maintain a good climate for growth and an invigorating forward momentum.

> *Self-actualizing individuals (more matured, more fully human), by definition, already suitably gratified in their basic needs, are now motivated in other higher ways . .*
>
> Abraham Maslow

If you want to get completely motivated and excited, energized and stoked, if you want to act as God would and transform your every fault into a virtue, there's one simple and extremely effective way to get the ball rolling and keep progressing—Prayer. **Prayer is the most effective way to help spiritual growth**. There's no single action that does so much for a sincere heart.

By asking God to help you and your friends, you're asking to be supplied with power and transformation to make yourself more spiritual. There's no inner problem prayer can't address. Prayer is the key to spiritual supply and acts to keep the channel of communication between yourself and your Father open, free, and clear.

When you pray, pray for transformation, not things. Pray to be a better person, not for a result, and trust that the best outcome is the spiritual transformation of God. Ask this for yourself and others. If what you ask for is God's will, it will happen, sooner or later.

Another factor of growth is Responsibility. I've mentioned complexity and the need for simplifying life and part of this strategy is to slow down and provide an environment that allows growth without feeling overwhelmed, which reduces pressure. This isn't merely reducing stress (Stress is normal and good in the right amount.) but reducing a level of *decision-making* you can't keep up with.

Try to control the amount of responsibly you take on: It's silly to expect to perform well with greater responsibilities if you can't handle the little ones. Our success isn't measured by how much we do, but by how we conduct ourselves. There's no shame in taking it slowly because quality, not premature quantity, is the key to a normal rate of development.

A further way to foster growth is by having a place conducive to spiritual thinking. If you can live with a mate, friends, or roommates who aren't adverse to your spiritual living, you can go home and get recharged and enjoy meaningful conversations. Sure, we should seek to help everyone, but please surround yourself with true friends who believe in you, because if you don't you'll end up fighting battles at home as well as on the outside!

Curiously enough, a frequently neglected element of spiritual growth is power, a critical element. I've already mentioned prayer as the most important source of power, but now I'll mention some sources you already know. Take time to play, laugh, run and sing, dance and shout, allow for a free expression of the eternal child attitude of trust and purity. Get together with friends and socialize; take trips; get outdoors; go out on the town; go to a show; walk in the park; go out to dinner. And, take the time to relax, letting the stress in your body flow out in some activity. Let the mind be free. Play.

And finally, take care of the shell that transports you through life and houses your Spirit of God, your body. Eat right, exercise, and pay attention to maintenance through care and the treatment of disease. Put it all together and get ready for *unlimited* sources of renewing strength and power, the requirements of life and eternity.

This person hasn't forgotten play:

> The thing that's probably the most fun right now is just being with the family on fun things: We've been going for a lot of walks and hikes. Just being out with the family and the dog Sierra, is just a wonderful feeling, the beautiful surroundings, watching Sierra romp through the forest and Hanna (our baby) kind of like seeing everything for the first time.
>
> We do it just because it's fun and we enjoy being together as a family.
>
> I also play tennis. I find that very renewing because I'm a very analytical person and the work I do is very mental and very analytical. In tennis you're not really thinking but reacting. It's physical; it's fast moving. And I find that to be tremendously fun. it's challenging because I have to push myself to play well, playing a lot against myself.

While we nourish ourselves, it's imperative we realize our thinking and attitude problems. There are many obstacles and distractions in the growth process, among which are prejudice and ignorance. Prejudice blinds us to the truth and crystallizes our actions into prescribed patterns; we lose the function of seeking truth. And if we choose to be ignorant, we won't learn how to keep growing and we'll also fail to understand our fellows.

Since conflict is normal and expected in any relationship or friendship, just imagine the effect of prejudice. In disagreement or conflict, or other trouble, we simply avoid any change since we believe we're right. Eventually, the good will and trust of the association is eroded away to the point of no return with the only perceived solution being to begin with someone new. These two attitudes are tantamount to avoiding the truth. Everyone should strive to seek the truth no matter what its source and be unafraid to apply it in all relations.

Along with prejudice, selfishness also destroys friendships and blocks the Spirit's light. If we fill our minds with selfishness, there'll be no room for the entrance of the touch of God, kindness. Consequently, we trudge along grasping for anyone and anything that unluckily gets within range. Through failure after failure God is still with us, but He can't get through the brick wall of self-absorption and ego-gratification until we accept Him and live for others, until we end sin.

We sin when we know we're going against the Father's will. Many times we make mistakes and don't know till later, but the conscious decision to avoid doing right is SIN. Continual sinning destroys our self-awareness (our soul) and gradually shuts the mind and heart off to God's Spirit. The result of such determined rebellion—iniquity—is destruction of the soul, complete nonexistence, total unconsciousness.

The idea that God metes out punishment is a human concept. When we feel wronged, our response is animal preservation and defense, the destruction of the threat. This is not God's way. God responds to acts of sin to preserve our eternal existence because the Creator isn't filled with anger, vengefulness, or bruised feelings, but with a total love to help His children. God's response to sin is a gentle hand or a stern voice, whatever gets through.

Ultimately, we literally destroy, blight, efface, cut down, or turn off our souls through acts of determined sin. At this point we don't live after death or we actually end the afterlife we began after death. In the latter case, God simply dissembles the empty shell which once held a person and returns it to the cosmos. This result has been our choice; we knew what we were doing to ourselves—complete self-destruction, cosmic suicide.

However, everyone sins, some more than others. After all, we aren't perfect and are naturally stubborn once in a while. Please don't be unduly concerned with your status before God, but also realize it's possible to destroy yourself if you set out to go against the Father's will. Just remember that if you're sincere, God understands, and that total spiritual death only occurs *because of repeated self-destructive rebellion*.

So, the key to effective growth is establishing daily habits that meet your needs. Build into your day simple habits, activities or little actions that give you the strength and direction to move forward in this world of demands. It may be that you'll exercise for thirty minutes after work; it may be that you wake in the morning and make a list of things to do; or it may be that you plan to speak to at least one friend.

A healthy habit is something you do each day or week that helps you grow by meeting a physical, mental, or soul need. Whatever it is you decide, make it simple, start out slow, keep it small, and keep it going. Learn to cultivate these beautiful patterns and see the wonders of effective spiritual living—doing the Father's will.

We must also not forget our bad habits. I define a bad habit as anything we repeatedly do that removes us from God and brings dissatisfaction and unhappiness. As all-consuming and endless as these compulsions may seem, they can be replaced by spiritual habits because the power and satisfaction of the good is much greater than indulgence, fear, or laziness. Good habits replace bad habits like vegetation replaces manure.

So, allow God in; let Him help you grow. If you want to become more than you are, brother or sister, you must act *vigorously* with God in displays of the Spirit. The improvement of your character only occurs by doing something, not merely refraining from the wrong. Our Father expects us to use our gifts in a celebration of cosmic destiny through a sublime service to each other.

You'll receive everything you need if you seek it.

Fruits of Growth

Returning to the aspen tree we purchased, how can we discern its progress? We know the tell-tale signs of height, green leaves, and good white trunk color. What are the characteristics and traits of a growing human reaching up to God? We'll find that it's quite apparent and simple, just as with the tree. You can find clear and fresh signs to gauge your progress and growth while being able to apply the same method to others.

If you're becoming like God, you're growing, expanding with eternal momentum. Our Father requires and expects us to do something with our lives, something *spiritual*—to grow. When your life begins to fill with love for your brothers and sisters, growth is flourishing in your soul. When you go out to help others with no personal gain in mind, you're moving in harmony with God. When this service envelops your life, you'll feel you've grown and be able to look back on your first awkward service steps and appreciate your changes. Not only will you relish these experiences, but you'll yearn for them.

Happiness will be ever-present amidst the strains and fears, the failures and accomplishments. Your mind will enjoy a flood of peace and assurance that the Creator is watching out for your spiritual welfare, no matter what horrific or frustrating situation you'll have to go through.

This person describes the experience:

> It's kind of like a feeling of being in balance where everything is in proportion and in its place. There's a balance between doing something that feels like it's productive and being helpful to other people and having a positive affect on other people and at the same time in a light way that it is fun and renewing, and is satisfying to myself.
>
> It's a feeling that things are right; things are in balance; things are in proportion. Everybody's benefiting from my actions, that my actions are making me happy and also having a positive affect on the people around me.
>
> I try to be there for friends when they need me and help them in a positive way. I have a very good friend, one of my best friends here who had cancer and had to deal with it on a short-term basis. We were able to get together. He really wanted to spend some time discussing his options. I felt that I was able to kind of really, really hone in, put myself in his place. I was able to focus and really get a quick handle on what it was that he was dealing with and give him some feedback that I think he found really helpful and really appreciated. That made me feel really good that I could support him and give him some good input.
>
> That strengthened our bond as friends that I could give him that support. I know likewise that he would give it to me if I needed it. It's a feeling like being able to be there for somebody else. It's very uplifting.

It's true that your life isn't going to be a blissful land of spiritual pleasure, but you'll be happy and touched by God.

Our lives aren't a constant high or mountain of successes, but often a set of demanding uncomfortable experiences acting as merciful teachers. Our happiness is found in the growth of our spiritual selves, not only the pleasures or ease our animal selves want. This is possible to the degree we give our lives to God.

If you feel something is right or true, how will you act? Will you do something or let someone else take care of it? What are your responsibilities in this newfound world of the Spirit? We all react differently to what we know we must and should do. As we approach the true levels of high spiritual living—dynamic and spontaneous growth—we'll immediately take whatever action necessary based on our values and ideals. We'll seek to do the Father's will in the best way we know.

Eventually you'll think and act according to what you know is right, your dedication to seeking the truth and living it. **You'll let no thing, man, or woman block your way** as you strike out on a course to independent spiritual living, a life of honesty and courageous action. Your only guide to truth and guidance, evaluator and tester of right, guide and counsel, will be the most qualified being, the Universal Father.

This is leadership, a life of sublime greatness and nobility for everyone.

> *I tell you, my friends, do not fear those who kill the body, and after that have no more that they can do.*
>
> Jesus, from *The Bible*

> *Be strong and of good courage, do not fear or be in dread of them: for it is the Lord your God who goes with you; he will not fail you or forsake you.*
>
> Moses, from *The Bible*

The challenge of others is the challenge of yourself: You have unrefined animal tendencies and bad habits disrupting your excellence in conflict resolution, personal achievement, and service. Therefore, another result of growth will be your complete mastery of these things—the ego. You'll so desire to become like God, bad habits will fade. You'll loose desire for them when they're replaced with spiritual actions. Every time you act spiritually, you're replacing a detrimental habit.

When you associate with people, you'll seek to serve them. Differences of opinion will be worked out with great tact and tolerance, not by passivity, acquiescence, or destructiveness. When you try to enlist the help of others, you'll get better at unifying everyone for a common goal since you understand their needs and problems. All this will be accomplished by understanding other's beliefs and behavior.

You may feel your problems are too many and much too complicated, but when you take the continual steps of growth, you'll learn how to work with problems as *welcomed* tools for growth. You'll see that these difficulties are the very experiences necessary to attain a life of freedom and happiness: Those of us who are protected from the challenge of life don't know its joy.

You'll also relish transforming personal fears or misunderstandings. There'll be no failure or defeat because these are the blessed and cleansing allies of spiritual growth. God wants you to do what you think you can't.

Forward you'll go by the power of your decisions and your Spirit's leading to embrace new worlds of discovery with changed living and understanding. Your world won't change, but you will. Onward, onward with glory, courage, and industry, onward with fearlessness and action you'll tread the high plains and rugged mountains of spiritual achievement. Nothing will stop you! God is with you! Your destiny is greatness! Your destiny is change.

Growth Difficulties

To begin and continue this undertaking entails overcoming obstacles. These habits and attitudes are real and constitute a tremendous challenge requiring total dedication and stamina. It's up to you and only you to overcome them.

We're at the beginning once again, back to our weaknesses. All of us have natural survival urges, defensiveness and selfishness, not to mention prejudices and preconceptions about life and people. Always, the animal tendency is to see differences as threats, to fight back and isolate, to live in fear and inaction. *The only way to overcome this universal problem of fear, dislike, and hate is by embracing our Father's attitude.*

Therefore, when you see people who are different from you in appearance, beliefs, and actions, remember they're sisters and brothers, who, like you, are on a journey of growth, who, like you, are imperfect. Understand these fellows and learn to love them; learn to help them.

This love for others is the basis of growth since we can't serve God when blinded by ignorance and fear. *Love everyone*; love intelligently; do something for someone that really helps, not merely satisfies an immature want of theirs; do something to help them grow.

> *It must also be clearly understood, that only such service to our fellow-men as really tends to increase their happiness can be truly called kindness, and all encouragement of idleness, dissipation, crime or vice, far from increasing the happiness of either the object or the subject, has precisely the opposite effect upon both, upon the one directly and upon the other sympathetically.*
>
> Oscar Newfang

Well, if we're supposed to love other people, really serve them, how do we do it? Since the process of love means releasing the Father's love, we must open our minds. After we know we're children of God and all people are relatives, we've got to seek to understand them. When you *understand* a sister or brother, there'll be a natural outpouring of the Father's love; you'll be compelled to serve them.

When you understand others, you'll no longer have feelings of hate, but forgiveness, and thus enable yourself to feel more of God's love for you. As a channel of God's love, experience it flowing to the effective ministry of others and love your friends and neighbors, everyone you see, as yourself. This type of love is the best ethics you could have, for it's based on real understanding and divine wisdom. And finally, when you love your fellow mortals, you'll seek to serve them, and in so doing, grow.

Here's a testament of forgiveness:

> Forgiveness. Forgiveness is a big one. Because people always do things: In the course of life they trespass against you; they step on your toes; they invade your space; they, ya' know, hurt your feelings, whatever. And there's plenty of opportunities to forgive.
>
> My brother and sister-in-law had done some very unkind things to me and hurt me very deeply. They took advantage of me; they took *sore* advantage of me and we had other conflicts. They came to my house over Christmas; they stayed for two weeks. They never offered me any money. We tried to have presents for all of them under the tree. They went out and spent all of their money on Judy's family, had nothing, not even a little token for the kids. But they went out and spent all kinds of money on Judy's family because they had, quote end-quote, limits, dollar limits on all the presents they could exchange with her family, nothing for me, not even a "thank you."
>
> Probably, gee, five or six years went by and I hardly spoke to my brother and his wife. I just had really hard feelings, really hard feelings. And I was standing at the "Peoples' Fair" when my little niece Jenny, Frank and Judy's daughter, came running up to me, just *so happy*

to see me (She was probably six or seven at the time.). And she came running up with her arms open and said "Aunt Alice! Aunt Alice!" She threw her arms around me and I hugged her and she hugged me. And I immediately started to look around for her mom and dad, because I knew, of course, that they must be nearby.

And there they were, standing across the aisle . . . And Judy was looking at me with this look on her face . . . I'll never forget it: The look said to me "I love you too! And I want you to love me but I can't because you don't love me." The look said "I wanta come over too and I wanna be with you too. But I can't because you don't love me, because you hate me." And I said to myself "Who am I to hold this person outside the circle of my love? Who am I to do that to her? No matter what she's done in the past, who am I to not forgive?"

And I made up my mind that I would forgive her for whatever she did, and forgive my brother. And accept them both, love them both just the way they are, and let them be who they are, and let them grow up and change, do whatever they have to do to be more godlike . . . I couldn't be better than God: God loves this person. Who am I to say that I don't.

So that was a real valuable lesson in my life because that look (You know they say a picture is worth a thousand words.), that one look communicated a thousand meanings to me. More than anything she could have said. That look communicated so much. From then on that was a turning point in my life because I forgave her. I truly forgave her. I never had the same attitude about her again. I never talked badly about her to anybody.

And now she's a dear friend of mine. I love her. I can honestly say I love her with all my heart. And she loves me. And I turned that relationship around. And that's a real treasure. That was a real service to God, but any time you do a service to God, you do a service to yourself.

This is the job, to let divine love fly through us to those in need—everyone. When we do this, we become like God. We grow.

Let's go forward together. Let's be our true selves. Everyone who responds to the divine leading will grow. Can we believe what's been done to us? Can we comprehend the glory and outrageous achievement awaiting us? We're blessed with the gift of the ages, the continual renewing of the Spirit.

Every personal problem can be solved!

There's no ideal you can't achieve eventually.

There's no person you can't love.

Let us grow!!!

Spiritual Truths

We must have spiritual priorities to grow.

We must give all to our Father.

We must constantly make spiritual decisions.

We must do our Father's will.

We must nourish our growth.

Happiness and eternal life is
the fruit of growth.

Love

The Attitude of Our Father
Chapter 10

○

The other day I got off the phone with a good friend. After small-talk, the conversation changed as she told me about her sister who had a sick diabetic husband who was in danger of losing both kidneys. Her sister decided to donate one of her kidneys to her husband, thus requiring protracted tests and an extended period of recovery.

I sat and paused . . . I can remember doing good things for friends in need, but this heroic act challenged my displays of love. I began to think, "I pray I can develop a love this deeply!" I think with God's help, everyone can.

The stuff and substance of our progress are the unimagined services of devotion to those around us. A life of growth is a life of matchless and enduring love for all our brothers and sisters.

The Need for Love

I believe everyone can agree that practicing love is a worthy personal and societal goal. Nonetheless, we're witnessing a world based increasingly less on the ideals of love which we inherited from our cultural and religious traditions. In light of our current social alienation crisis, we should be concerned with the alarming disintegration of bonds that once unified us.

Relationships and family interactions are the best indicator of the general malaise. If you talk to most friends, they have a family or friendship story of frustration or estrangement which began with simple disagreements that accumulated to the breaking point. We must face reality and be humble to the fact that our current attitudes toward others are inadequate and destructive to our happiness and civilization's progress. All of us should let go of the fantasy that we don't have any problems of significance affecting our friendships and families: It's not the other guy; it's every guy. Unfortunately, most of us exhibit a misunderstanding of love and its application.

Just a glance at the creeping plague of ill feelings and fragmentation should be enough to show even a disinterested person we can't continue our staggering gait. Each of us is the architect here. Our ways of relating give birth to a tension and gnawing fear which will increasingly disrupt and disturb our world if we fail to change ourselves—every individual. World change is started by looking in the mirror and across the dinner table. We need to start making these personal changes now!

These people illustrate our common weaknesses:

> I tend, at night time, bedtime, the kids' bedtime, to get cranky. I want to get them to bed; they're always putting up delaying this and that and the other thing. My temper is shortest right at that time of day. And so very often the prelude to getting them in bed turns ugly. Sure, at the end it's always prayers and everything's fine, but getting them into bed, it's just my temper that's the shortest at that time of day. They sense it, being vultures, and they jump in and *stretch* it out.
>
> I very easily get caught up in the power struggle of that moment, rather than looking at the long-term, trying

to figure out a way to do that where I don't lose my
temper; there's no distancing. It's difficult. I deal with
that all the time.

I guess there's been times when I've gotten angry
for selfish reasons because of trying to get my own
agenda through in a situation. Probably the person you
interact with the most, at least if you're married, is your
(spouse). I think it takes a real effort to keep the special-
ness of a relationship, keep the freshness as time goes
on.

Sometimes I think it's easier to get angry when you
have that familiarity with the person as opposed to if you
were in a new relationship. I think there's a tendency to
be more tolerant because the relationship is building. I
think that's an unloving act at times, to take relationships for granted and not treat the person with the same
kind of respect that you would, someone that you didn't
have that same degree of familiarity with.

Most of us are sincere. Therefore, our current crisis is of
the mind, not the heart, and is born of misunderstanding God
and the spiritual life, the life of love. Insidiously, each of us
has been drawn back into the primal selfish survival instincts
and pleasure pursuits; most people in this age have devoted
much time and energy to denying and avoiding problems,
seeking pleasure, and attacking others. We can't run away.
Everyone is affected to some extent, no matter how small.

*Without God, without religion, scientific secularism
can never co-ordinate its forces, harmonize its divergent
and rivalrous interests, races, and nationalisms. This
secularistic human society, notwithstanding its unparalleled materialistic achievement, is slowly disintegrating.
The chief cohesive force resisting this disintegration of
antagonism is nationalism. And nationalism is the chief
barrier to world peace.*

The Urantia Book

While confusion and fear reign, again I believe it isn't a motivation crisis; it isn't that we've lost our desire to be like God and love our sisters and brothers, but rather we're confused by the destruction of religious and moral foundations that gave rise to humankind's progress; we've outstripped our religious understandings with an over-emphasized scientific world view.

The path to a better world is the path of love-vigor, the living of true love. Nothing else will work. We should know, we've tried everything else.

The Definition of Love

Along with the loss of traditional religion's roots and accompanying moral understandings, was the loss of the concept of love itself. Very few people have a rock solid idea of love and how to live with it because it's been distorted and misused. No amount of sincerity or hoping will cure the sores of misunderstanding and dissatisfaction unless a person strives to comprehend love.

We must also note that our entire understanding of love is dependent on our understanding of the Heavenly Father—God. Once we understand the nature of God, we're given a model to imitate. Without this model, the effort is fruitless.

Love is the attitude of God, our Father, the Creator. This is God's wonderful unending persistence to do everything necessary to help us find cosmic passage. Perfection is His way, the ideal of love. From infinite efforts, through many years of trying, overcoming every obstacle, your Father and mine does what's necessary.

God delights in loving and being loved and without restriction or qualification; there are no strings attached; God loves unconditionally!!! Everyone is invited by God to fulfill His plan. We do this with God's way—LOVE.

When a person helps another to live the Father's will or meet a simple need, that person's done good. *Love is the desire to help*, to do something good for someone. To our best understanding, we can strive to do simple things that help others on the road to God. If we act with love, we help, rather than merely satisfy another's unrealistic want or selfish urge. The real way finds what's best for a person, seeks the challenge, overcomes fear and anger, and transcends mere animal survival priorities. When we act with love, we do something for someone that helps him or her! That's our only concern.

If we take a careful look at services done with love, we'll realize they, like God, are true, beautiful, and good. If you can describe your actions in one or all these ways, you've acted with love, the ancestor of the qualities of God: truth, beauty, and goodness. So, it's clear that actions not giving rise to any of these three things aren't done with love.

Love is the way of God, therefore it's spiritual. *This is the test of your spirituality or religion*: Are you growing in your desire and ability to love everyone as God loves you? Love is spiritual behavior. Anything said to be spiritual which doesn't exude love isn't spiritual. Love is the clothing of a child of God seeking His will.

> *Just as a flower gives out its fragrance to whomso-ever approaches or uses it, so love from within us radiates towards everybody and manifests as spontane-ous service . . . When we feed, clothe and attend on anybody, we feel like doing all these things to our own body, for which we do not expect any return or praise or commendation, because all bodies are our own; for, we as the all-pervading Atman or Spirit reside in all bodies.*
>
> Swami Ramdas

Compare this ideal with common notions of love. Love in no way seeks for personal gain, but God's gain. If you act with love you'll approach every relationship to help the other grow. This is a tremendous alternative to the world's confusion in this regard, because countless people seek to use others to fill a void with pleasure-seeking or control.

When you're filled—electrified and motivated with God's love—you come with such spiritual *abundance* that the other is in turn compelled to love you and God. Here there's no selfish attitude but a realistic and mature devotion only to the growth of the other.

Scores of us grab another person for the wrong reasons, the selfish and fearful reasons. Frequently we look at another as a need filler, much like going to the store to buy food or clothing. If we are distorted and confused we want to control others to make them do what we want, to live out our fears and fulfill self-centered inclinations.

This woman illustrates many of our pitfalls:

> My first husband, obviously since I'm now divorced, was an unhealthy relationship. You know, co-dependent: They all are. The relationship was unhealthy because I wasn't a balanced individual and I was looking for balance from him. I was getting what I needed to complete myself from him.
>
> One of the things that was wrong with the relationship was that I had no structure in my life and I was very young and he was very structured. I plugged into his situation and he sort of kept me structured. In the meantime he really made a lot of choices for me that I should have been making for myself and I *knew* I should have been making for myself. But I also knew that by doing that I was compromising my integrity. In the moment that it was happening I would know that I was making less effort than I would normally have to.
>
> I was not utilizing my personality the way that I should've. I wasn't taking risks that I normally should have been taking by making decisions. So, I was sort of sliding along easily not having to take responsibility for my life. But in the process I was also losing my integrity and my self-esteem. So, even in the moment that it was happening, even though I knew that I was sort of being

> bossed around, I still knew that I was getting a tradeoff
> for that by not having to take responsibility for my life.

In contrast to this situation, a person with real love comes to celebrate a mutual partnership in the adventure of growth and service to share a *common goal*. These people act with unity and strength as mature adults of a loving Father. Here there's not the slightest thought of controlling another's decisions but rather a habit of inspiring and enlightening, learning and appreciating the other.

This leads to a relationship where negative emotions, fears and angers, laziness and apathy, are gradually replaced with an impassioned enthusiasm for living and discovering the thrilling solutions to life's problems and goals. When a problem comes, it's a welcomed, a cheered *opportunity* for becoming like God.

People living true love act with fresh honesty, firm devotion, and a matchless loyalty to the ideals of friendship. Every obstacle is overcome in a triumphant journey to deeper and deeper levels of intimacy and common expressions of living. The two lovers or friends are willing to do everything necessary to benefit the other's growth: telling the truth, being patient, trying to understand, and even saying goodbye. Love will go to every length necessary. With a love unlimited, a friendship is unlimited.

Aspects of Love
There seems to be no end to what love influences or the expansion of its domains. Love is everything for the spiritual life; it's our ideal.

When you step forward and give your time, forego a pleasure, overcome anger or fear, or benefit someone in another way, you've stepped into the supreme experience of living. Love is greatest because it flows from the Father *through* us and encompasses the universe. Taking the step to understand a person's problems and helping solve them is the other half of the purpose of existence in addition to the pursuit of personal goals; this is what we're about.

I Shall Not Pass Again This Way

The bread that bringeth strength I want to give,
The water pure that bids the thirsty live;
I want to help the fainting day by day;
I'm sure I shall not pass again this way.

I want to give the oil of joy for tears,
The faith to conquer crowding doubts and fears,
Beauty for ashes may I give always;
I'm sure I shall not pass again this way.

I want to give good measure running o'er
And into angry hearts I want to pour
The answer soft that turneth wrath away;
I'm sure I shall not pass again this way.

I want to give to others hope and faith;
I want to do all that the Master saith;
I want to live aright from day to day;
I'm sure I shall not pass again this way.

Ellen H. Underwood

If you haven't known this thrill and mystery of serving, you haven't known God or life. How can any other experience or achievement match the majestic rhythms of a life of endless unlimited living love?

Deep inside you burns the Spirit, your personal, individual friend and guide. If you feel this Spirit friend (awakened to the Father's touch) your life will begin to fill with acts of love. When you go beyond self-bounds to serve other selves, you have the Spirit within and have provided proof that you've responded to God. Who but the divine Spirit working in soul and mind could transform inherited animal tendencies into great and mighty acts? The Spirit is the source of God's love to you: You can show this same love to others to create value for them and yourself.

Without doubt, everything of lasting value comes from God's attitude. Just take a look at the beauty of the country-side, plants and animals, smells and soft sounds and appreciate that they exist because of God. In the same way, we live love when we create the true, the beautiful, and the good. Love is creation.

Our intelligent creation services are evidence of true religion, a good understanding of spirituality. It's up to us to inject the power of love into our religion whether we participate in an organized religion or not. If our religion is valid, it impels us to touch as many of God's family as possible with the ministrations of the Spirit.

You're deluded if what you call religion doesn't tell you to love everyone, enemies and strangers, as well as friends, with the same devotion and intelligence. We're *pioneers* of a new tradition of religion and spirituality for the purpose of sympathetic understanding, acceptance and service: The Universal Religion. We are trailblazers of ideal personal relationships.

Love is person to person and the best way for two people to get along while also being the highest motivation to meet the solitary challenge of frustrations and confusions. There's no problem two people who love each other can't solve. The success of any relationship is dependent on the degree of dedication each person has to the Father's Will—unconditional love.

When you feel love for another and sincerely seek understanding and insight, you'll be rewarded with the knowledge of how to help him or her. When you have the motivation of love, God will give you everything necessary to help. Your desire of love is the key to open your mind to God. Love is the secret ingredient of every successful association or endeavor for good. When you and your coworkers do a worthy project and it succeeds, it's because, in some degree, at some point, on the whole, you've loved each other and the people you serve. Love produces the finest civilization. Many people don't realize our world was built on the long road of painstaking trust and love. If everyone lived as God would have them, our society would slowly change into a heaven on earth.

Let's take a look at these women and their commitment to each other and their ideals:

> I have a girlfriend that came from a totally different background than me and we have pretty much come together in common because of our spiritual beliefs and the fact that we both have children. She is a good friend: It's a healthy relationship because she makes it known that regardless of what I say to her she will try her hardest to understand my point of view, even though it may be different from her own. She's very loyal.
>
> She listens for anything in my voice that tells her that I need to see her if I call her up and say "Well I just thought maybe we could get together today," even though she may have a lot of things to do. She's sensitive to my needs. So if she hears something in my voice, she will make it happen, not just maybe, sortof, kinda. She's always there and she always lets me know the things I'm doing right.
>
> The things I'm doing wrong she just sort of blows off, unless it's something like serious. She's very forgiving. Another thing that makes it a healthy relationship is not only is she very unconditional in the way that she looks at who I am, but she also trusts me with the problems in her life that no one else knows about or she feels she can come to me and just dump a lot of things. I will help her uphold the values that we both agree are important. If she says "Oh my husband's such a jerk.", I won't say "Well, you should have divorced him a long time ago." Instead I'll say, "Yea, husbands are like that." Then I'll suggest something that might help get them back on track again. She does the same thing with me.

The biggest thing about it is it's based on agreed upon values. That makes it healthy because we hold a certain level of communication and ideals in common that we don't stray from. We know that we both hold it so neither one of us are allowed to digress into something that is less than what we both hold to be important. It's a nurturing sort of thing for both of us in spiritual growth and as individuals.

It's not easy to love this way because there's a natural resistance to going beyond basic survival efforts. When you come across someone who's physically attractive or charming, it's simple to nurture feelings of love. But, the *real* test of love are those we find unattractive, disgusting, selfish, irritating, and hateful. In addition, people you find hard to love are the people who need your love the most, and the enthusiasm and persistence you apply to loving these people indicates your closeness to God. When you realize your life is filled with loving acts of service, you can say you're becoming more like God.

Therefore, regardless of the situation or person, **the only valid spiritual reaction is love**; despite what someone's done to you, love is the best way. You should always be willing to do what's needed to help a person know God. This doesn't mean you do whatever a person wants you to do or that you waste words on unwilling listeners, but if you think you can help someone know God, you should. This is a superhuman feat!

Projecting and flowing His power through us, God has the unlimited ability to achieve His plan. Love is the power of God, the greatest power, but it can't be measured or weighed, tasted or manipulated. Nevertheless, it can be felt. God's love is real and courses through our spiritual veins in an enduring glow and desire to serve, transforming every part of our lives.

What is there that God's love can't do? What crushed soul can't be raised up to be a child of God? What problem can't be used to free a person from limitations and fear? What experience is unable to bring love? When you experience the Father's love, when you feel your divine parent, you're compelled to give His love in return, to attempt to do the seemingly impossible.

We are the children of God. Everything's possible with His love.

While it's easy to get enthusiastic, we must realize learning to love is like any learning: We've got to suspend old notions and then imitate new patterns persistently. After a great amount of practice, the ways of love become second nature, almost unconscious expressions of our intent. So let's give them a shot.

Loving God—Reacting With Love

Our goal, let's not forget, is to know our dear Creator-Father. Giving our love to God is eternally linked with giving our love to others, our reactions to human need. This means we must let the divine love flow out when and how it's needed.

Our minds and souls are windows to the world of the Spirit. The more like God we become, the more we know of Him and experience His presence. This entails using (to the best of our ability) God's gifts for helping others. Love is doing something for someone they need done: God needs us to do His will to fulfill His plan. Loving God is helping Him with His plan and knowing Him. Knowing God is serving others.

As with any person, by helping God we're loving Him, cooperating with the burning feeling to become perfect through service. When we dedicate our will to the Father's will, the clear light of our Creator pours into us with knowledge, feeling, and power. *We must help God first to experience Him more.*

It's only natural we feel love for our Father who gives life and the possibility of eternal life. The Universal Father comes with ultimate love, a boundless generosity that elicits in us a desire to give it back by sharing it. It's because God is so good and fair, kind and understanding, that we love Him and do not fear Him. When you learn the true nature of God, you have a desire to love Him in return. God is the most lovable being throughout the universe because He is so wonderful and because He loves us.

To know God, we must love Him. To love Him, we must help others. Coming to know God and experience Him in a widening sense is wholly dependent on your dedication to doing His will, *the only gift you can give God.* We're part of the Father's eternal plan, a necessary part of the mysterious outworking of universe creation. The only way we can love God is by doing what He wants us to do, finding ways to make ourselves better people by helping others. Participation in God's plan is the greatest privilege. To think, we simple humans can contribute to the purpose of the universe!

Although you can't see God face to face or understand how and why you can love Him, it doesn't disprove the fact that you have a relationship with Him. God, the greatest experience, is a real person whom you can know. The passport to life with God is the adoption of the divine will, the life of love. And as you thus love God, you gradually learn to love as He does.

This means you *react* to need the way God reacts to your needs, immediately, spontaneously, and unconditionally. True love doesn't wait. When you forgive another, the Father's love is released through your being, and hopefully fires you to higher levels of service. This means we don't wait to give our love and act immediately, at the best time.

This husband clearly understands the phenomenon of immediate love:

> When Nancy was in labor, she had a real difficult labor. I think that I was as much there for her as I've been and could be. Basically, anything that she needed I tried to help her out with, whether it was getting a doctor or trying to comfort her, assure her, or whatever. I think I was really there for her.
>
> With my daughter Hanna also, we try to respond to her, to be there for her pretty much instantly and not say "Well, let her cry for a few minutes because I'm in the middle of this." Usually, I try to really be there for her as much as possible.
>
> And I think for friends and family members, I've helped out a lot of people: My expertise is in financial matters. They've come to me for help with a financial question. Usually I try to help them out, even if somebody called me and I just wanted to relax and read a book or something. Instead they called and needed a half hour of my time on some financial thing they have goin on. Usually I'll be there for them.
>
> I won't say "Well, I don't feel like it now." I guess I feel that if someone asks me for help I'm usually quick to respond. It's important for me to feel that I'm the kind of person who is there for whoever needs me. I try not to judge it and say, "Well, is this person important enough to me that I should spend this effort now." I try not to do that. I try to have the attitude just to be there for people as much as I can.

This is the beginning of greatness. The more we emulate the Father and His love, the greater we become. The love of the Father is tender, merciful, peaceful, and selfless. As the Father is, we should be sensitive and responsive, understanding and sympathetic to the difficulties of our earthly family members. This means we don't simply pass by and ignore the people we *know* we could help. Each of us has to choose whom we can clearly help.

There are many I can't help that you could, and vice versa. We have to use intelligence to guide service impulses to do real good rather than fading impulsive gestures. Find where you can be most effective and apply the power of your experience and gifts to bring lasting good change. If you can't do this, you must question your real motivations. But, it's always better to err on the side of doing good.

Looking at someone who's wronged you or is experiencing the pain and confusion of his misdeeds, forgive and then show mercy. Don't withhold what could bring a brother or sister closer to God, even if this person's hurt you or themselves, because all of us rely on our Father to be merciful when *we* demonstrate sincerity. If a person sincerely seeks to improve himself and his or her relationship with you, how could you censor your love and support? What reason could you give for letting them linger in darkness? At one time or another all of us have been there and required a helping hand and a loving touch.

> *He who forgives, and is reconciled unto his enemy, shall receive his reward from Allah.*
>
> *The Koran*

> *Then Peter came up and said to him, "Lord, how often shall my brother sin against me, and I forgive him? As many as seven times?" Jesus said to him, "I do not say to you seven times, but seventy times seven."*
>
> *The Bible*

While many people say, "That person's getting what they deserve and should be left to feel pain alone," we should view this as an opportunity when this person's mind is *open* to spiritual melodies. Look at these moments as boons to doing the Father's will, as wonderful adventures in merciful forgiveness and stunning transformation. Believe in God's love and mercy for yourself and you'll believe in your mercy and love for others.

Another way to react to need is to be a peacemaker. The result of a materialistic, nonspiritual life is violence and restlessness. To the person who isn't leading a spiritual life, this world is an enemy which must be subdued and destroyed to ensure personal survival. Life is filled with endless pressures and potential failures, a gloomy sky of black smoke, eliminating the sun. These people don't live peacefully: They're filled with a restless searching to satisfy their spiritual needs. The problem is that they try to fill these needs by material means, leaving only confusion, frustration, and pain. Just look at our world.

When you find these people (You won't have to look far.) realize they're needy, crying out. Be a maker of peace and lead them to satisfy their spiritual needs with celestial power and philosophy. Bring combatants together using inspiration and faith and emphasize their *unity* of purpose to achieve the common good. Look at your friends and make peace; look at your family and make peace; make peace with the world.

God doesn't stop until our necessities are filled, so we also must learn to love this way. We should never end the outpouring services required to spark the heart of a friend to the heights of spiritual brilliance. Go the second mile as God does, willing to suffer anything to help, to wade the waters of persecution and abuse for the living ideal of love.

Love means you have something to give and that you respect yourself. If you don't have this respect, you'll never be able to persevere through the bitter trials of opposition to your service. Many don't like loving service and try to destroy it out of fear or selfishness. Stand firm and gain your self-respect from the fact that you're a child of God who's becoming eternal by this very service and willing to die for your beliefs. If you have this devotion, you'll live forever.

Our Love exists because we have relationships. The great rewards of living are these joys. When we demonstrate the reactions of love, we're building tremendous friendships that'll last forever. It's this spectrum of friendships and relationships that makes life worth living, creates the real goals and rewards of existence, and gives strength for the adventure of becoming more and more like God. Problems shrink; disappointments become tools; pain begins to fade; hope is born anew, all from the benefits of loving friendships. There's no greater service than a friend for a friend. We're here to help each other.

How to Love

Many of us want to be idealists to take up the challenge of the Spirit, wanting to love and do it effectively, but how do we do it? What do we need to do to find the Father's love and give it? What are the doors that must be unlocked and with what keys? We have to answer these questions to be better lovers.

How can we be expected to act with this superhuman devotion and service? Isn't this a bit much? The fact is, God *expects* this love from us since He's placed it in us. What excuse can we dredge up to avoid loving someone in need when we realize this? What reason can you give for not bestowing the love of the gracious Spirit that envelopes your mind? We should remember that the Spirit is absolutely unlimited and can assist us in any way because it is of God. Everything we need is right inside us.

While we take joy in the Spirit's power, to dip into the endless supply of love we must spend time with God: If we never go to the storehouse, how in the world can we expect to get any of its riches? If we never take the time to ask God for help and listen to Him, how can we expect to do the same for a desperate friend? To become Godlike, you must bask in the love of God and vigorously give this fruit of the Spirit to another person.

This interview shows the importance of prayer and worship:

> It helps by getting things back into perspective. When we're not acting in a loving manner it's because we've lost perspective on what's really of value, what the real goals here are, all of those things; we're out of perspective, particularly with people we're close to. We don't have any trouble loving the world, it's loving the people who are close to you that's the problem. That's because we lose perspective from the wear and tear of daily living, the problems that come up and stuff. And that's when we start acting in an unloving manner.
>
> It requires stepping back into prayer and worship to regain the perspective. *That's* what's essential. It also gives you the time to recollect the energies to plot strategy, if you will, in terms of how to react. It helps you to gain perspective; it helps you to gain energy and gives you a way to work out your program, your corrective strategies or whatever.
>
> There are realizations that occur in prayer and worship that can help in all kinds of ways. It's very difficult to get that aside from prayer and worship . . . those are the best times for it and quite often the very thing you absolutely need to have: You can't think through it; you can't . . . whatever. You've got to create that opening for the Spirit to be able to speak with you. That's the best way to do it.

Trying to love and grow without spending significant time with God is like trying to learn to read without the alphabet or its sounds. *Each of us has to maintain the vital connection with our individual Spirits of God.*

This is the source of the unselfish desire to do good. No other source of inspiration can match the perfect power and tender touch of God. We only fool ourselves when we substitute reading, talking, etc. for real time spent with God.

The only way to live unselfish service is to know God, love Him and in turn love others.

Interestingly, once we've spent time with God, we encounter a new problem: How do we release God's love, and when? No one can just go out and help another person without understanding their actions and the genesis of their problems. Once you understand their motivations, there slowly flows the kindness of sincere devotion and tolerance, not before.

Men and women have the same general needs and problems, but react differently and explain these reactions differently. It's by understanding these explanations of conduct that we're able to see their sincerity and commonality of existence, the response to needs. And when you realize that your fellow is seeking God also, nothing can stop the Father's love from impacting him or her through you, even if you don't understand the other person fully.

Seeing others as on the spiritual path brings new dignity to them and concern for their welfare. Understand that all people were created by God for the same purpose, to do His will and grow eternally. Allow yourself to see their potentials while here on earth, even though they may make ridiculous mistakes and do cruel things. Cultivate forgiveness, sympathy, and acceptance of their current state—a natural step along the way. Most everyone wants to become a better person. Discern them in this light and you'll have allowed God's love to come through you.

In trying to love another, there are many factors, but the surest way is to serve. Allow God's love to come through you and you'll realize you're developing a friendly affection, a blossoming loyalty. So many people think love is an autopilot. *If you want to really fall in love with someone, work hard for their spiritual welfare.* As time goes on, you'll love them deeply and bring them to God by the power of your actions, and in the end, this is the greatest thing you could've done for them.

> *When we extend our limits through love, we do so by reaching out, so to speak, toward the beloved, whose growth we wish to nurture . . . In this way the more and longer we extend ourselves, the more we love, the more blurred becomes the distinction between the self and the world.*
>
> M. Scott Peck

People will value you as a friend and seek to be with you if you exude genuine friendship-love because they're *hungry* for it. Sadly, many believe that it's simply something you find or unearth. How wrong! Real devoted friendships are founded on unity of purpose, similarity of interest, and a mutual desire to love unselfishly. Friends work through all the difficult times, through fear, anger, and pain, to help each other grow.

All in all though, most of us are sick of hearing about love. While love is one of the most overused and abused words, and we are a bit jaded, it remains a beautiful ideal to strive for. Love is the attitude God has for us and the secret of a successful spiritual life. The fact is, *we exist to love.* What would life be like without the possibility of loving and being loved?

We're charged with love to go outside our egos and conquer fear and anger with strength. After everything we've looked at in the preceding chapters, love remains the most accurate characterization of a spiritual person.

In the end, God wants us to have the greatest experience we can, His love. Therefore, look at others as God looks at you and treat them as God treats you. Understand this world needs loving spiritual living above all. Stand up to every conceivable hatred and malice, withstand every calamity and pain, transform yourself. Let's bring our lives and civilization into the unity of God's will.

You can do it! You can love everyone! Take a risk; touch a heart; give a great service; believe in a friend; be a friend to all. *Expect* to find the best in everyone and you'll find the best in yourself as well. Here I challenge you to release the endless fountain of power God places in you: He wants you to touch those around you.

Love is the greatest part of life. Be unafraid and believe your life can make the difference! Go out and challenge the world with the strength of your convictions and the steadfastness of your devotion. When everything says "no," risk all for God's love. Believe in yourself and God.

God is depending on you. Use every day as an adventure to love as many as possible. Find someone who's bothered you, even angered you, try give understanding and cooperation. Push through every personal boundary and travel the domains of spiritual expression and meaningful living. Know the pain of others; be sensitive. See every day as a blessing where you may bless and act with faith, effort, and courage. Do the impossible! Heal the wounds and let the strains of spiritual music dominate your life. Be kind in a life of great nobility and join the vanguard.

We're not talking about a life of ease, but rather a life for the spiritually tough, persistent, and courageous where you surmount your greatest fears and survive to be an example. Love does everything needed: confronting a friend, speaking the truth, teaching a child, cleaning filth, helping the sick, putting in extra effort, overcoming the ego, etc. **In fact, living the Father's love is the most strenuous and rewarding statement you can make. Let us not forget that the loving application of our Father's will to the fullest requires tremendous and ever-increasing faith, effort, and courage.**

So my friend, dare to trust and grasp the dynamic thrill of real love. Let go of everything holding you back from the destiny of service awaiting you. You are a child of God. There's nothing that can stop your love—God's love. Allow God to love through you. Allow God to love you.

Spiritual Truths

Love is our Father's attitude.

Love is the desire to do good to others.

Love is the greatest relation.

Understanding service to another
will create love.

We exist to love.

When we love, we experience
our heavenly Father's love.

The Answer
of
Answers

The Key to Spirituality
Chapter 11

O

I am sure you've heard most, if not all, of what I've said before. Indeed, the great religious minds have given me a challenge and inspiration to write and accent eternal truth. But, owing to the complexity and overwhelming noise of our civilization, I must stress that the value of the truths I've shared is in their conscious selection, emphasis, and use, above the cacophony of life. It's in this last chapter that we'll learn the most important answer, the secret of spiritual success and eternal life.

The truths we've examined are the foundation of a spiritual life. The secret of satisfaction and progress is in believing and using these facts. A spiritual regeneration in your life and humanity is absolutely dependent on recognizing, understanding, believing, prioritizing, and living these truths!

In any endeavor, getting the essentials is extremely critical, much more so with life. Let's say you want to be an excellent carpenter. Imagine you've shown up at the job site without skill in hammering or using a nail gun; consider you don't understand how to level a floor or cut straight; try to see yourself building this house without plans. Eliminate the essentials of this trade, forget about your needs, and you'll be stuck on the ground with a pile of lumber and nails.

Try to nurture a garden without water, teach a child without books, or cook a meal without an oven; try to keep warm without clothing, hear music without musicians, or breathe without air. You could no more do these than you could be happy without knowing and living the truths we've studied!

This man knows the purpose and crux of life:

> I think understanding the spiritual essence, if you will, and finding the connection, is probably the most important thing there is . . . There are three things that happened to me, and they all happened within a month: My wife and I decided to get divorced; I went through a business setback; and the net result of those two things is that I found myself living in a motel room. I had no home; I had no wife; and I had no job; and I had no office. It was a real humbling experience, probably the *best* thing that's ever happened to me.
>
> . . . I was wandering around in a state of shock. And then, all of a sudden, things just came together, like they had *never* come together before. I'm in a really different place than I was six months ago.
>
> There's no question that finding that spiritual connection and living the essential truths of whatever your inner voice is saying to you or whatever it is you live in concert with, you've grown up with, whatever spiritual path it is that you ascribe to (And there's a number of spiritual paths out there that have connected with them essentially the same morality.), is the most important thing there is. And anybody who's not doing that is missing the boat.
>
> One of my favorite quotes says the most important thing in your life is to find what that inner voice means

to you and follow that leading. I think very few people in our society today are able to quiet their lives enough to do that.

What happened to me in that motel room is the fact that I got rid of the distractions of business coming in one ear and family problems coming in the other ear. I finally got quieted down for a period of time and able to get back to some real grounding that I've never had for twenty or thirty years. I had to get to the point of being totally naked, or totally stripped of almost everything before I was able to go and open enough to let that happen.

I knew intellectually that spirituality is the most important thing. But until you get it at a feeling level you haven't got it. You have to go through a disillusionment with whatever the other paths are that you're trying to follow, usually unsuccessfully. Some people cling to those other paths *all* their lives and they never take the opportunity to be introspective enough to go really examine what life's all about.

Most of us believe we can get along and be happy without the spiritual essentials, like our interviewed friend. But, only by responding to our needs and spiritual poverty can we seek the better way as the Father's liberated children. *There's no other way or solution.* We've tried everything else. Now it's time to realize our personal and collective destinies.

The Answers

Our future as individuals and a species is determined by living the teachings that follow. Yes, we've already looked at them and heard about them, but our problem exists world-wide and individually because most fail to get it. Many superb religious leaders have graced us, but their truth was always buried in the world's confusion. It's our responsibility to study, live, and teach these truths despite the confusion and cultural interference. Let's look at the truths that comprise The Universal Religion, with our mission in mind.

Be ye . . . perfect, even as your Father which is in heaven is perfect.

The Bible

If, after having been born a human being, one give no heed to the Holy Doctrine, one resembleth a man who returneth empty-handed from a land rich in precious gems; and this is a grievous failure.

Gampopa

✳

Happiness and an eternal destiny can be yours!
Please understand, believe, and accept the fact that you can live your dreams, a world of happiness, satisfaction, and noble greatness. Come on! Get up and thrill with the knowledge; yell and jump; clap your hands and dance; allow flowing tears; delight in a sparkling smile. All great things of the spiritual can be yours! Friendships, achievements, endless adventure and mystery, and the Father's love are yours for the asking.

You can live forever in this friendly universe with possibilities for overcoming and improving, growing and learning, that are endless by design. How could we envision a more blessed and tender future? Traveling and studying, loving and helping, finding and celebrating glory in the universe with God is our eternal voyage. All the ambitions, drives, needs, ideas, projects, everything you couldn't realize here you will find *out there* if it's in accord with God's plan.

Your change will be stellar and total assurance from God will be your staple. Nothing will harm you spiritually; no one will stop you on the quest for the Creator of the world and all other worlds. Your life will be filled with triumphant courage and exertion for others and yourself.

Can you see the infinite possibilities even here on earth and know what glories and successes await the next day or week? Can anyone imagine the infinite? Your greatness and joy can begin this minute, in this room, or wherever you are. God weaves us into the glory of His masterpiece. Our lives are meant to be progressive. God is love.

✳

You are a child of a perfect Father-God!

The *person* who makes everything possible is your Heavenly Father. You are a child of God with all it's implications and opportunities. Think . . . Think what this means for yourself and everyone. Your ideal of a perfect God is merely a faint shadow, a fading light, compared with God's actuality. Therefore, eject every negative idea you have about God and start experiencing Him as a loving Father. This is the best and only way to understand Him.

You're a child of God because you're a person as God is a person and have His Spirit. Attempt to feel the personal hand of God reaching through Spirit. God's made it possible for you to exist because He's given you your personality-self-consciousness and allows you to recognize that of others.

Our Infinite Father has planted self-consciousness in each of us. Everyone is a unique individual expression of the person of God; every soul on this planet and in the universe is different. All the sweet relationships, experiences, and satisfactions are yours because you're a person. All thanks to God whose child you are.

✳

You can have a relationship with God!

Despite the fact that we can be just plain stubborn, God wants us to get to know Him and share our lives with Him. At one time or another most of us have fallen in love and felt its joys and pains, believing this was the greatest experience. How silly and shortsighted when we realize the Heavenly Father is always trying to establish a one-to-one Father-child relationship with us which is far more satisfying and reliable.

God is a real person and therefore gives the pleasure of communication and friendship with Him. Like infants, we gradually move toward a fuller understanding of the world and our parents. It's the same between ourselves and God. Our Father loves us so intensely that attempts to describe His love are always inadequate.

Be comforted and enlivened, the Father of all puts a piece of Himself in you to know you and for you to know Him. Through every moment in the long difficult path, your perfect friend can always be relied on. God wants you to eternally choose to know Him as well as He knows you. Be happy! Be thrilled! Be electrified! Be rejuvenated! You've got a friend who can meet all your needs and help out and won't leave under any circumstances. You've got a real friend in God.

You can become like God!

Think a moment about your identity and lifestyle and try to determine what portion of your life is controlled by outside negative influences or mind problems. All of us are filled with imbalances and other confusions and bad habits. Nevertheless, recalling this, remember that the spiritual wins: You'll become more like God if you desire and work hard. There's nothing you can't overcome since the Spirit can transform you. But, you must allow it to.

Cooperate with your Spirit to become a person who'll live forever and love as God. And remember that while your Spirit transforms you, realize your sincere service can electrify those you serve. The spiritual life always transforms the world and yourself.

※

All people are your brothers and sisters!

Since everyone's created by God, we're all related. When you go out in the street, understand that those who share that street also share the Creator. After you accept that you're a child of the Creator you realize all others as family. There can be no strangers now. All of us are people and hold the individual Spirits of God within and are involved in a resurrection and the God search.

To make everything work with the Father's will we should be united in a concert of effort to contribute to His plan. We're required to work in groups and ever larger groups. How could we go through life knowing God and not acknowledge that all of us, however varied in culture, politics, or learning, are His children? Hold this thought daily and treat everyone as you would treat your closest family member, friend, or child. Love as God loves, as a parent.

※

God cares for you as a person!

The universe's vast population is unknown, but we can be absolutely assured that God knows each person one-to-one and wants him or her to know Him one-to-one. Our loving Father puts our progress as top priority; each of us is cared for as though we were the only one in creation. Everything we need for our spiritual lives is provided for.

God listens with an eternal ear of compassion and attentiveness so that you'll receive what you need long before you know you need it. You're given as many opportunities as you need to transform into a living, growing, eternal daughter or son. God sees you as a unique, lovable person and He'll do everything for your spiritual welfare.

*

A piece of God is in you!

God delivers endless kindness by His individual Spirits. Every time a human being shows he or she could benefit by a Spirit friend, God sends one. Inside you lives just such a Spirit of God, the eternal promise of growth and communion with the Father, the companion of forever.

This guide helps you become more spiritual as you decide to respond to its leadings. A direct link to God, your Spirit teacher takes you through life's lessons and counsels you in divine solutions to problems. Your friend is compensation for your humble start and will continue with you forever if you choose.

*

Your greatest satisfaction will come from serving others!

A dynamic tendency constantly seeks to lead you to service. As you begin to respond to this leading you'll discover that serving others is a blessing and that bearing these Spirit fruits brings sublime peace and joy, unlike mere survival struggles.

Life will be translated to eternal glories where service opportunities are met with enthusiasm and used as a tool to know God. You'll look forward each day to service as the greatest satisfaction as other activities will diminish and recede. In the end, you'll look back and wonder how you could've lived without serving.

✳

All spiritual experience is yours if you're sincerely trying! You must realize, God is fair and knows your intentions. If it's your intention to respond to His leading, to become like Him, to help others, to do His will, He'll go to every length to help you achieve these intentions. God will take you along every step, especially those you didn't dream existed.

Let's face it, God knows everything about us, our identity, needs, and destination. *You're not judged by what you've done but by what you really want to become and accomplish.* Therefore, your Father views you with an eternal perspective, seeing who you'll be while listening to your heart and understanding your struggle.

When you feel the urge to find the truth and act to sincerely discover and live it, everything necessary will be given to you. The very fact that you respond to the urge of God means you've become capable of enjoying His endless spectrum of gifts. No other requirement is needed to start and continue the journey. If you're sincerely trying, everything will be alright and you'll know the joys of eternal life.

The Key of Life Eternal

Now it's time for us to look at the secret of secrets, the joy of joys, the gift of gifts. Without this knowledge, life is a meaningless torture test of despair and frustration, but with it we're children of an infinite glorious destiny, the Father's children. *This is the most important fact humanity can know* . . . So what's the key?

**You determine your reactions to your experience
and determine what you'll become
and whether you'll reach your destiny.**

God's given you life—freewill self-consciousness. Your
existence requires that you constantly make decisions, even
though you may not want to. Your decisions and actions
determine your thoughts, what the Spirit can teach you, what
you'll experience, and whether and how you'll grow.

This person speaks of the value of freewill:

> We would have to say "What would it be like not to
> have freewill?" I believe that as you get older you
> become conscious, if you mature right, of a greater and
> greater degree of that freewill: You are exercising more
> and more of it. It means two things: It means you have
> a tremendous adventure/risk here because you not only
> have the opportunity for growth, but you also have the
> opportunity for stagnation and for destruction.
>
> The more I'm conscious of the ability to act, the
> more I'm concerned that I act in concert with the
> ultimate will of the Father so that the end product is the
> right one, I think it's kind of intimidating to know that.
> It's also humbling. It's also exciting to know that one
> can affect one's own destiny.
>
> The more one is able to exercise freewill, the more
> one notices how seldom it's exercised by other people.
> Just seeing people make the same mistakes you've
> made, and doing the same things you did, and abso-
> lutely, *totally* sure that they're doing the right thing . . .
> you see them on a, kind of, personal ego-trip. You know
> that you've been through that and you've tried to do
> that. And the ultimate way to develop is through service.
>
> You look at people doing that and you realize they
> think they're operating free, but there's always that alien
> presence with them. So, when you sit down to have a
> normal conversation, a free and happy conversation with
> them, you always feel that that brooding over-ego is
> always there.
>
> The way I find it most successfully exercised is
> when I am in tune with the Father. Each day I need to do
> this. When I do not have intention; when I begin a day or
> activity without intention, without a definite plan,
> without definite intention for a result, if I start a day and

I can't say "This day I want to achieve these particular things" when I fail to exercise that, I fail to exercise freewill.

What I do is start reacting to what's in front of me. When the phone rings I react to that situation. The way I exercise it now is by trying to put the stamp on the day at the beginning, trying to develop an intention, trying to have an intention when reading a book or having a conversation, and not to waste time doing things where I don't have an intention. You can have an intention just to enjoy yourself or watch something silly on television or read a book that's light. Whatever intention you have is fun. Make sure that you're doing *that* and not just in a state of reacting to whatever confronts you.

Considering the significance of the divine creation, we realize that everything is a gift, even the freewill we use to enjoy our other gifts. The hunger for truth, the desire to know God and others, the desire to serve, the ability to think, our gifts and talents, all these we can affect. Potential . . . potential with a focus of freewill is the best way to describe us.

Everyone, even if identical in gifts and experience, would turn out differently because God gives us a choice. We aren't manufactured parts at a cosmic factory or puppets in an eternal farce. How complete and wondrous is life, the gift of using gifts, the gift of deciding what, why, and how to act. While God gives the potentials and raw materials of life and future destiny, we're the architects of growth. It's up to us whether we use what we have or throw it away.

There's no influence that can force you to change your intentions. This is sacred.

And while we relish our gifts, we must remember that they aren't just for bliss and ease; our Father requires that we respond to the urge to help others. Our Father wants so much for us to go forward and follow the eternal path He provides for our adventure. The needs that burn in you, the urges of God, determine that you must do something.

When you do something, you'll be held responsible for your real intentions. There's no way to escape responsibilities: These are the results of living and making choices. Fear not! God knows what urges you wish to respond to and what you desire to happen.

Each of us is custodian of our gifts. Our beings are filled with great urges to become like God and are simultaneously given the truth needed to satisfy these urges. We're constantly bathed in the love of God along with other tremendous rewards. God expects us to take care of these gifts and not selfishly exploit or discard them to get our way.

Your Universal Father will ask what you did with your treasures. He will respect you with mercy and kindness in accord with your true, selfless intentions. If you don't respond to anything God's given, you will destroy yourself. In the end, you'll lose your ability to even exist.

Keep your chin up! don't be afraid! So many of us were taught that God is looking for opportunities to punish or hurt us, scare us, that we find it hard to accept the reality of His love. Our Heavenly Father is so kind, fair, and gentle, that it's impossible to fail if we desire progress!

My friend, you've been given the power of freewill— decisions. The more you use this muscle for doing good, the stronger and more invigorated you'll become. Power, energy, and enthusiasm are added to you by God's Spirit as you tune in to God's will and become a conduit for His might. Imagine it! The Creator's mandates coursing into and through you, giving you partnership with God, giving you life. *This is the secret of spiritual stamina, of boundless, endless endurance and performance.*

The perfect man is a spiritual being. Were the ocean itself scorched up, he would not feel hot. Were the Milky Way frozen hard, he would not feel cold. Were the

mountains to be riven with thunder, and the great deep
to be thrown up by storm, he would not tremble. In such
case, he would mount upon the clouds of heaven, and
driving the sun and the moon before him, would pass
beyond the limits of this external world, where death and
life have no more victory over man; —how much less
what is bad for him?

Chuang-t se

Every time you act spiritually on a desire to meet a need, solve a problem, or attain a goal, you're given spiritual **power** and **enthusiasm**. Feeling this way means you're feeling good, feeling spiritual. As a decision is made it gives rise to the desire to make more decisions which in turn provide more power and inspiration.

When you're tired and depressed, the easiest way to rise up is to make a decision to do something positive. Immediately you'll be given power and love if you accept it. This is the joyous cycle of a living, breathing, glowing child of the Father. No one can use this privilege for you; *you must exert yourself with faith, courage, and persistence.* Life and happiness depend on your actions to keep your part of the cycle going.

As you begin to make more decisions to live the spiritual life, you'll be given periods of rest. But soon new meanings and challenges will emerge to beckon you to greater responsibilities and decisions. Your new levels of achievement will set before you a row of decisions that must be made to reach the next level. It's through the mastery of these levels of decision-making that we gain new heights of spiritual experience and joy. Decisions are the key.

Beyond the Words

Now we know the answers, the truth about God and ourselves. So many times we've been here, filled with new ideas and light. It's time to act on what we know. Let's allow ourselves to be lead and do all, release all. What possible reason do we have for waiting? Let's jump up and claim our lives now. It's coming to us, the moment of action.

Feel the truth expanding in your heart and know the promise of the future. Be sincere and open your mind to the glories meant for you. Learn to spend time listening to God's voice and acknowledge the longings you've had for so many years to be a better person and help others, the unending longings to know God.

When and as you *feel* these supernal truths, let them touch your mind by the sincere seeking of your heart. Accept the excitement and understanding of life and God that's opening in you like a colorful flower, or a river rushing. Refuse to keep denying the urges and truths that've been emerging in your mind. Don't allow the prejudice of others to withhold the greatest experience of a human being. Believe.

Nothing is more important if you want happiness. Believe in God and then learn to believe in yourself. In this age of doubt and dark sarcasm, of over-sophisticated and confused materialistic philosophy, know that the real truth can't be withheld from you. Believe that you'll triumph.

This person knows that spiritual triumph is our destiny:

> Just saying those words gives you a feeling of peace, peace of mind. If you really, really know that ultimately you are going to triumph spiritually, that's a peaceful feeling, a kind of a secure feeling. It's some-thing that we have to keep telling ourselves over and over and over *and over and over*. I for one am the type who is never really satisfied with where I am spiritually. I think that I *should* be doing better, being more spiritual, being more like God.
>
> Even though you know that, ultimately, yes, you are going to make it to heaven and get a lot more help than you've got now, that's a nice secure feeling. At the same time you have a feeling of really wanting to try

harder and do more than what you're doing. Even though I know that I have chosen to do God's will, and I keep choosing God in my life, I believe the promise that, yes, we will triumph spiritually.

But it's very hard to take that into my psyche. It's not that I doubt or despair, but I just feel like *I'm coasting*. I need to work harder. I really want to make this time productive and look back and say "O.K., I did a good job down there on earth." I don't want to just relax and know that I'll be saved. I want to do good things for people. And I want to do things that will last longer than my life, have a good positive impact on the world when I leave it.

There's something within us that wants us to really try to be more like God right now, here and now, and not wait for heaven to progress, but to struggle with this very human mind and very human body and try to really make the most of it.

I think it's good when people can really take that to heart, that they will triumph spiritually. That is the faith that dissipates fear. Faith is the antidote for fear, and I really find that that holds up. Whenever I get into a fearful mode I can ask for more faith. And that faith is that yes we are in God's hands, yes we have an eternal career. It's always good to get that cosmic perspective, knowing that yes "I am surviving; yes I have an eternal career; I will triumph because God has created this incredible myriad of beings who are gonna help me all the way up."

Right now is the most difficult part where we need more faith. And we have more faith than we even cash in on. When people really get that and take it to heart, they will really triumph. It gives them a freedom from fear and also a hope that's like a balm, a *soothing* balm. They can go out and smile and look at a tree or a cloud and *just* relax because we're all so in a hurry. And if we get our cosmic perspective I think that we start taking more time to enjoy our lives.

Look in front of you: I'm not talking about some unattainable prize. God places the gem in you now and all you need do is look at and accept what you're *already* experiencing. God is your Father, and you His child. Joy can be yours. All of us are brothers and sisters. This is a fact as obvious as the blue sky. We shouldn't deny or pull back from it.

Believe in yourself and your ability to know the truth. Look at what's happening inside you, the undeniable truth, and don't allow yourself to be slowed by any reason. If I go outside and see the sun, I know it's there, warm and good. When you allow yourself to see God's presence, there's no need to discuss or argue. If someone stays inside on a beautiful day, how can anything be revealed to them? Every person will eventually believe in the existence of a loving Father-God if they are sincere and not confused.

Have faith. What you seek will be found. You'll see spiritual sunshine if you come out and look. Be persistent and triumph in the birth of the Spirit. This process may be sudden or take time, but eventually you'll know God if you try long and hard enough! Come join the family.

I promise success if you're sincere. If I shook your hand you'd feel it. If we stepped out and viewed fireworks, we'd seem them. And think: All these are secondary experiences outside us. If we look inside at primary experiences, we'll see what's already happening, God's love.

Some of us were taught that God isn't a person, only a set of physical laws. I know that I am, yet I can't scientifically prove it. I know that God is and am glad I can't scientifically prove it! I tell you, more real than any object, is God's smiling face. Most young children will naturally express a belief in a loving God because they're simply relating what they experience and know. Many of us have lost this simple trust and honesty but if we approach God this way, we'll hear and know Him. By sincere patience and persistence, your faith will show you who was always there.

*"Let the children come to me, do not hinder them;
for to such belongs the kingdom of God. Truly I say to
you, whoever does not receive the kingdom of God like
a child shall not enter it." And he took them in his arms
and blessed them, laying his hands upon them.*

Jesus, from *The Bible*

In any study, profession, or trade, we're constantly told to work hard and pay attention. If you're to begin and come to believe you're a child of God, you must give full dedication to listen for Him and live with Him. Your purpose is to do the will of He who made us. Give everything for God in a display of selfless love and appreciation and seek spiritual priorities with total enthusiasm and dedication. Do this daily and learn to sanctify life with the nobility of sublime service.

Sit down with God and share what you truly wish from life and want to become, mention your feelings and what you think. Thank the Creator for everything you have. Sit. Silently listen with total concentration and sensitivity, be persistent, and in time you will recognize and know God daily. The more you talk to God and sincerely listen, the more you'll know Him and help Him help His family. Come with the trust of a child.

Please remember God needs you. You can give God the intelligent use of your gifts and talents for serving others. You have dignity! You have God's respect, confidence, and support! I thrillingly inform you, God knows your intentions and is ever patient with your struggles and mistakes. Greatness awaits you; you have unlimited potentials of spiritual achievement.

*What dignity of destiny and glory of attainment
await every one of you! Do you fully appreciate what
has been done for you? Do you comprehend the grandeur of the heights of eternal achievement which are*

*spread out before you?—even you who now trudge on
in the lowly path of life through your so-called "vale of
tears"?*

The Urantia Book

**You are a child of a perfect Father God and we're all
His children!!!**

This statement is the most important utterance for all
time. We've heard it many times before, but its power is in
the belief and living of its meanings. Without this belief,
there's nothing, with it, all possible spiritual progression and
glory. The choice is yours.

My dear sister or brother, we stand at the edge of a
boundless universe of unending eternal spiritual discovery
and glorious adventure. Together we're off to experience
those things that will transform us into children of light. No
force can stop us on our rugged and long climb into the
universe annals.

This life God hands us is of maturity and strength, as
well as pleasure and bliss, pain and difficulty, as well as
success and enjoyment. Let's not leave it locked inside our
minds, just a sterile idea, but let it explode through shining
enthusiasm and balanced living.

We're the children of the Creator-Father working together
to realize better lives and a better world. We're God's
offspring who, when faced with problems and seemingly
insurmountable obstacles, look within and calmly do what He
asks. We persistently jump high with the assurance of
spiritual success even though we can't see the future, must be
extremely patient, must suffer occasionally, taste confusion
and anxiety, drink of death and physical pain, be occasionally
thwarted or opposed, experience criticism, and feel many
afflictions. And in spite of everything that says "Don't do it!"
we're willing to trust that the Father's will is the best for us

and everyone. This is our evolutionary greatness and the stuff of honor.

Our time is now, the next age of spirituality. All people will know their inheritance and potential as sons and daughters of the Universal Father. What can stop us? What life can't become a joyous spiritual expression?

I ask you . . . what limit can ever be placed on your spiritual development? Look inside: There's an actual piece of God the Father (pure spirit and pure energy) simply awaiting your decision to start. Think now of your greatest fears and frustrations, pain and hardships, but also your dreams and ambitions. Whatever you think will stop you from achieving life with God, simply remember *it can't*.

Your life has meaning and purpose. You're here to experience this difficult life to become a spiritual child of God who'll live forever. There's no other way but to resolutely and bravely overcome all impediments, fear, hatred, malice, disease, and death. Shine your light.

> *Having started out on the way of life everlasting, having accepted the assignment and received your orders to advance, do not fear the dangers of human forgetfulness and mortal inconstancy, do not be troubled with doubts of failure or by perplexing confusion, do not falter and question your status and standing, for in every dark hour, at every crossroad in the forward struggle, the Spirit of Truth will always speak, saying, "This is the way."*
>
> The Urantia Book

Go out, noble child of God, fellow traveler, be a real adventurer and pioneer, a risk taker, a bold force for good. Be willing to do anything for God and devote your life to knowing Him and serving your universe kin. Let nothing stop you. Let troubles be opportunities, allowing yourself to grow in their cleansing, strengthening challenge. Dare to live for

God's will. Dare to understand, forgive, and love everyone. Dare to follow the majestic path of righteousness up into the glory of the mysterious and wonderful country of God.

Welcome!

May our Father's will be done!

The Absolute Truth

God is.

To learn more about *The Urantia Book* contact:

The Urantia Book **Fellowship**
529 Wrightwood Ave
Chicago, IL 60614
Toll Free (877) 335-5669
Email: ubinfo@ubfellowship.org
Web Site: www.ubfellowship.org

The Jesusonian Foundation
POB 18764
Boulder, CO 80308
Toll Free (800) 767-5683
Email: ubooksrus@aol.com
Web Site: www.jesusonian.org

About Revelation Publishing

We hope you've enjoyed this book.

Revelation Publishing provides books of illumination and inspiration influenced by *The Urantia Book*.

We recognize and respect the value and dignity of each person and their right to choose personal spiritual beliefs. We respect everyone's spiritual and religious expressions and hope that the books we provide will be useful and inspiring in your life.

We send best wishes for your spiritual explorations.

You are a child of God. We are family.

Order Form

Revelation Publishing
Books of illumination and inspiration.
You are a child of God. We are family.

Telephone Orders: Call (800) 474-7109 toll free (U.S. and Canada), local and international (302) 292-6875. Have your credit card ready.

Fax Orders: (302) 292-2963, Send this form.

Postal Orders: Revelation Publishing, POB 7136-UR1, Newark, DE 19714-7136, USA (302) 292-6875

Web/Email Orders: www.revelationpublishing.com

All books may be returned for a full, unconditional refund.

Quantity   **Amount**

_____ *The Universal Religion,* **$14.00**   _____

Total number of items _____

U.S. Shipping & Handling: $4 first item _____
            $2 for each additional item

International Shipping & Handling: $9 for first item _____
            $5 for each additional item

Enclosed Coupons or Discounts ⁻ _____

AMOUNT ENCLOSED (U.S. Funds) _____

Name: _____

Address: _____

_____

City: _____ State: ___ Zip: _____

Phone: _____

Email: _____

Payment: ❏ Check/Money Order   ❏ Credit Card:

❏ Visa,   ❏ MasterCard,   ❏ AMEX,   ❏ Discover

Card number:

Name on Card: Exp. Date: /